PRIVATISATION STRATEGIES AND TECHNIQUES

Privatisation
Strategies and Techniques

R.K. Mishra
R. Nandagopal
Ch. Lakshmi Kumari

ANMOL PUBLICATIONS PVT. LTD.
NEW DELHI - 110 002 (INDIA)

ANMOL PUBLICATIONS PVT. LTD.
4374/4B, Ansari Road, Daryaganj
New Delhi - 110 002
Ph.: 23261597, 23278000
Visit us at: www.anmolpublications.com

Privatisation Strategies and Techniques

First Published, 2004

ISBN 81-261-2034-7

PRINTED IN INDIA

Published by J.L. Kumar for Anmol Publications Pvt. Ltd., New Delhi - 110 002 and Printed at Mehra Offset Press, Delhi.

Dedicated to

Prof T.Navaneeth Rao

President, Institute of Public Enterprise
Chairman, Swamy Ramanada Theertha Institute
for Rural Development
Former Vice-Chancellor of Osmania University
Chairman, Education Reforms Committee,
European Commission
Who is a Constant Source of Inspiration to Management Teachers
and Researchers in Social Sciences

Contents

	Preface	ix
1.	SLPEs in India: A Overview	1
2.	Modalities of PE's Reforms and Privatisation of SLPEs	45
3.	Divesting State Ownership—A Tale of Two Companies	66
4.	Valuation of Shares of State Level Public Enterprises—An Illustrative Case	86
5.	Public Sector Reforms in Rajasthan—Reforms and Privatisation	97
6.	State Level Public Sector Enterprises in Maharashtra	108
7.	Outline of Activity of State Public Sector Undertakings in Orissa	131
8.	Privatisation and Non-Privatisation Reforms in State Level Public Enterprises: Sectorwise Strategy and Implications	143
9.	Non-Privatisation Reforms in State Level Public Enterprises (SLPEs)	188
10.	Less Government or More Government?	198
	Bibliography	206
	Index	222

Preface

The performance of the State Level Public Enterprises (SLPEs) continues to remain a puzzle. They have been responsible for a substantial chunk of subsidies offered by the state governments. The second generation reforms aim to reduce the subsidies given by the states to their SLPEs in order to bring down their dependence on the Central Government. The present work makes an attempt to dissect the performance of the SLPEs in the various states and figure out the reasons responsible for their poor performance. An attempt has also been made to strategies the portfolio of these enterprises in the various states in terms of what should and what should not be retained by the various state governments.

The present work is based on the collaborative seminar organized by the Planning Commission and the Institute of Public Enterprise in 1992 at the Planning Commission. The Seminar was attended by attended by the policy makers from the Central Government, various State Governments and nodal organisations. The Seminar discussed the feasibility of non-privatisation reforms, restructuring and privatisation of these enterprises for performance improvement. The experiences of some states with privatisation were also discussed. It was felt that while non-privatisation reforms were necessary to bolster the performance of non-privatised enterprises, it was necessary to off load the perennially loss-making enterprises from the public enterprise portfolio in view of the continuously deteriorating financial position of the state governments.

We thank Prof.T.Navaneeth Rao, President, Institute of Public Enterprise and the former Vice-Chancellor, Osmania University for encouraging us to complete this study. He is a constant source of inspiration for researchers engaged in the study of social sciences. His support has fuelled our interest in research at the Institute which provides vital inputs to its consulting, training and teaching activities. We therefore, dedicate this volume to him.

We thank Prof.K.Harigopal, Director, Institute of Public Enterprise, for his encouragement and support in completing this venture. We also thank Ms.S.Lalitha, Administrative Officer (Research)for providing logistical support. Ms.J.Kiranmai has provided help in preparing the manuscript and we are thankful to her for the assistance.

We hope that the book would be found useful by policy makers, researchers and post-graduate students.

– R.K.Mishra
R. Nandagopal
Ch.Lakshmi Kumari

1

SLPEs in India : An Overview

Introduction

The State Level Public Enterprises (SLPEs) are an important component of the public enterprise system in India. According to the report submitted by the Study Group on Reforms on State Public Sector Undertakings set up by the Planning Commission (2002), 747 SLPEs had the total investment of Rs.1,97,105 .47 crore as on March 31, 1999. The Central Public Enterprises (CPEs) as per the Public Enterprises Survey : 2001-2002;Volume I numbered 240 with an investment of Rs.3,24,632 crore as on March 31 2002. The contribution of the SLPEs to the GDP is about 5 per cent as compared to 10 per cent by the CPEs[1]. The role of SLPEs can be assessed from the total turnover as a percentage of the Gross State Domestic Product. There was no consistent patter among states and this percentage generally varied from 1to17 per cent of the Gross State Domestic Product, with most states falling in the range of 6 to15 percent. Although SLPEs constitute 60 per cent of the total investment of the CPEs, they are three times the number of the CPEs. The average investment in a CPE was 5 times more than an SLPE. However, the SLPEs in terms of the resource use and control depicted a different picture as compared to their counterparts in the central sector in that they directly impacted the functioning of the state economies and had a greater exposure to the state political systems. The SLPEs are characterized by weak middle management systems as they do not have on their rolls the requisite number of professionally qualified mangers. The top management in these enterprises comprise mostly an IAS CEO and nominees of the state governments drawn from civil services, defeated politicians and political party in power.

The financial performance of the SLPEs bore the brunt of these shortcomings. Between the 1991-92 and 1998-99, the SLPEs continued to incur net losses and showed the chronic tendency of accumulating losses which trend continued to persist even in the case of nine states for which data are available for 1999-00 to 2002-03.

Methodology

The macro analysis provides in the beginning an overview of the SLPEs in India in terms of various financial parameters. The macro analysis incorporates data for all the state

1. Mishra.R.K., Restructuring Public Enterprises in India, Mittal, New Delhi, 2002, Pg.3

The macro analysis provides in the beginning an overview of the SLPEs in India in terms of various financial parameters. The macro analysis incorporates data for all the states from 1991-1992 to 1998-99 (abstracted from the Study Group on Reforms on State Public Sector Undertakings set up by the Planning Commission (2002)) . The macro analysis for the period 1999-2000 to 2002-03 incorporates data for the eight states collected from the primary source (i.e., financial profiles of the state-wise individual SLPEs obtained by the IPE). This is followed by a discussion regarding the privatisation scenario. The privatisation practices state-wise have been discussed to provide a birds eye view of the trends in privatisation in the various states. Finally, the commonalities and the distinguishing features of privatisation in the various states and as between the SLPEs and the CPEs have been studied to highlight the important developments and underscore the lessons that could guide the future privatisation efforts concerning the SLPEs.

The information for the study has been drawn from the Study Group Report on Reforms on State Public Sector Undertakings set up by the Planning Commission; the reports of the Comptroller and Auditor General of India (Commercial) pertaining to the various states; data format[2] circulated to the SLPEs, Chief Secretaries, Finance Secretaries and Bureaus of Public Enterprise of the various states; economic dailies; state websites; personal interaction with the policy makers and functionaries in the various state governments; and constant telephonic interaction with the concerned officials.

Total Investment

Table-1 shows the total investment in the SLPEs. About 80 per cent of the total investment was shared by Andhra Pradesh, Delhi, Gujarat, Karnataka, Maharashtra, Punjab, Rajasthan, Tamil Nadu, Uttar Pradesh and West Bengal. Maharashtra topped the table followed by Delhi, Uttar Pradesh, Karnataka and Andhra Pradesh. Each year the investments were shooting up by about Rs.15,000 crore. In 1998-99, the incremental investment were to the tune of Rs.24,127.69 crore maybe because it formed to be the opening years of the Ninth Plan. In the case of the nine states this trend in investment did not hold good in the case of states such as Kerala, Rajasthan and Arunachal Pradesh due See Annexure-2 to the closure of some of their SLPEs

Typology

Annexure-1 presents the sectoral distribution of the various SLPEs. It is evident that the manufacturing enterprises followed by the trading and services enterprises dominated the scenario. This was because the various state governments emulated the central government in giving a fillip to industrialisation. The trading and services enterprises received an encouragement to provide export thrust and create a suitable infrastructure of services at the state level. The promotional enterprises were set up to orient social activities with an economic tinge at the state level. The welfare enterprises were a new breed of the SLPEs set up to provide economic support to the backward classes of society, comprising scheduled castes, scheduled tribes, minorities, women and handicapped. The table indicates Andhra Pradesh, Assam, Gujarat, Karnataka, Kerala, Maharashtra, Tamil Nadu, Uttar Pradesh and West Bengal showed a preference for manufacturing, trading and services and financial enterprises whereas, Kerala, Maharashtra and Uttar Pradesh showed a preference for promotional and welfare enterprises. The preference for economic and social infrastructure might have been responsible for the respective choice. The utility enterprises had their presence in each major state. These comprised the state road transport corporations and the state electricity boards and in some cases, unbundled state power utilities-generation companies/transmission companies/ distribution companies.

Capital Employed

Table-2 represents the investments by way of net fixed assets and working capital . Such investments are financed by debt, equity and internal funds. The capital employed increased by about 160 per cent from 1990-91to 1998-99. The capital employed figure was only marginally higher than the total investment during this period indicating the lack of organic growth. Andhra Pradesh, Arunachal Pradesh, Kerala, Maharashtra, Mizoram, Orissa, Pondicherry, Rajasthan and West Bengal showed more than the average growth in capital employed of 160 per cent. Besides these states, Assam, Delhi, Gujarat, Himachal Pradesh, Karnataka, Madhya Pradesh, Punjab and Tamil Nadu owned substantial part, i.e., about 90 per cent of the total capital employed by all those states. For the nine states the trend in the growth of capital employed for the period 1999-2000 to 2002-03 was positive but the stock of capital employed generally measured lower as compared to total investment indicating imprudent use of investments.

Net Worth

Though the net worth showed the trend to increase manifold (Table-3), it turned out to be a shade above 14 per cent of the total equity which pointed to a negligible growth in net worth and erosion of shareholders basic capital in terms of real investment prices appearing to be a great cause of concern. The equity erosion occurred in Assam, Jammu & Kashmir and Nagaland. These were precisely the states where the subsidies accounted for major portion of the losses incurred. The happenings in the nine states for the period 1999-00 to 2002-03 did not present any antimony and the general tend continued to persist.

Total Revenue

This represents the top line of an enterprise. This provides cushion against contingencies and a cover to meet expenses. This should grow at least at a compounded annual growth rate of 10 per cent to set off the loss caused by the real rate of inflation. This should be at least 3 times of the investment. Table-4 shows that total revenues turned out to be a discouraging figure of about 59 per cent of the total investment. The total revenue comprised the income from mainstream operations and other yields. The total revenue scenario tells many untold facts of lack of marketing drive, quality consciousness and soft targeting. The states which earned more than average on a rupee of investment were only handful. In 1998-99, such states included Andhra Pradesh, Goa, Gujarat, Haryana, Jammu & Kashmir, Madhya Pradesh, Maharashtra, Rajasthan and Tamil Nadu. For the nine states for the period 1999-00 to 2002-03 the mixed trends were visible with J&K and Kerala showing continuous growth, Karnataka and Arunachal Pradesh showing continuous decline and U.P, Gujarat. Pondicherry ,Rajasthan and Goa showing mixed trends. The use of investment continued to remain poor in the case of nine states during the period 1999-00 to 2002-03 as total revenue-total investment ratio in terms of percentage was 38 per cent.

Net profit

Net profit is the be all and end all of all businesses. It is not only that top line is important for a business but it is also essential to see that the bottom line is positive. Net profit making helps in updating the technology, contribute to an organic growth and provide a unified direction. Net profit making is a vital aspect in general but more particularly to the telecom industry which is undergoing the motions of restructuring and merger. It adds to building up reserves and surpluses and higher earnings per share. The vast challenges of expanding the telecom networks to the rural areas and towns and providing value added services can be overcome through adequate profitability. Net profit making is the core element of corporatisation which takes place through the concept of equity participation, limited liability, setting up the strategic business units and practicing responsibility accounting. The operationalisation of these concepts create a harmonious internal environment where the different units/ product groups-services could compete with one another to improve their efficiency. Profitability strikes an optimum tradeoff between the demand side factors (revenues) and the supply side factors(costs) in a competitive regime.

The net profits should at least be equivalent to prime lending rate or 10 per cent of the revenues earned which is the bench mark prescribed in financial management. The Net profits for all the states taken together for the various years of the study excepting 1994-95 and 1995-96 were negative (Table 5). On the average, net profits for all the states taken together have been negative by around 1 per cent of the revenues earned. Assam, Delhi, Jammu & Kashmir, Kerala, Madhya Pradesh, Mizoram, Orissa and Tamil Nadu have been major net loss earners in 1998-99. The net losses incurred by these states not only wiped out the total profits of the profit making states but also were responsible for the phenomenon of loss making. The nine states did not show any deviating trend between 1999-00 and 2002-03.

Conclusion

A dissection of the macro-economic performance of the SLPEs clearly reveals that their financial performance continued to caused a great deal of concern. According to the Study Group Report on the Reforms in State Public Sector Undertakings for the period 1991 to 1998-99, instead of earning a 10 per cent rate of return, these enterprises registered a compound annual growth of 17.36 per cent in their net losses. The policy makers are left with no choice but to rethink about the retention of the SLPEs portfolio in the various states and decide what to divest and what to retain.

Annexure-1

Andhra Pradesh

1	A.P. Fisheries Development Corporation	P
2	A.P. Beverages Corporation Limited	M
3	A.P. State Civil Supplies Corporation	S
4	A.P. State Film Development Corporation	P
5	A.P. Forest Development Corporation	M
6	A.P. Handicrafts Development Corporation	P
7	A.P. Housing Board	M
8	A.P. Agro Industries Development Corporation	M
9	A.S.R.T.C	U
10	A.P. Foods	M
11	A.P. State Housing Corporation	M
12	A.P. Industrial Development Corporation	F
13	A.P. Industrial Infrastructure Corporation	M
14	A.P. State Irrigation Dev. Corporation	M
15	Leather Ind. Dev. Corpn.	P
16	A.P. State Meat Development corporation	M
17	A.P. State Mineral Dev. Corpn.	M
18	A.P. Minorities Fin. Corpn.	W

19	Nizam Sugars Limited	M
20	A.P. State Police Housing Corpn.	M
21	A.P. State Seeds Dev. Corpn.	M
22	Singareni Collieries Company	M
23	A.P. Small Scale Industrial Development Corporation	M
24	A.P. State Trading Corporation	M
25	A.P. Technology Services	M
26	A.P. Textile Development Corporation	M
27	A.P. Tourism Development Corporation	U
28	A.P. Urban Development and Housing Corporation	M
29	A.P. Warehousing Corporation	T&S
30	A.P. Urban Finance & Inf Corpn.	F
31	A.P. Road Dev. Corpn.	F
31	A.P. Infrastructure Dev. Corpn.	P
32	AP TRANSCO	U
33	AP GENCO	U
34	Andhra Pradesh Dairy Development Corporation	M
35	Andhra Pradesh State Financial Corporation	F
36	Allwyn Watches	M
37.	Southern Transformers & Electricals Ltd.(S)	M
38.	Allwyn Auto Limited	M
39.	Republic Forge Company Limited	M
40.	Andhra Pradesh Steels Limited	M
41.	Marine & Communication Electronics(India)Ltd.(S)	M
42	Aptronix Communications Ltd.(S)	M
43.	A.P. Essential Commodities Ltd.	S
44.	Hyderabad Chemicals & Fertilizers Ltd.	M
45.	A.P. Non-Resident Indian Investment Corpn. Ltd.	P
46.	Eastern Power Distribution Company of A.P. Ltd.(S)	U
47.	Southern Power Distribution Company of A.P. Ltd.(S)	U

48.	Central Power Distribution Company of A.P. Ltd. (S)	U
49.	Northern Power Distribution Company of A.P. Ltd. (S)	U
50.	A.P. Power Finance Corpn. Ltd.	U
51.	Andhra Pradesh Wind Farms Limited (S)	U

Arunachal Pradesh

1.	Arunachal Pradesh Forest Corporation Ltd.,	P
2.	Arunachal Pradesh Industrial Development of Finance	F
3.	Arunachal Pradesh Mineral Development & Trading Company	T&S

Assam

1.	Assam Agro Industries Dev. Corpn. Ltd.	P
2.	Assam State Film (Fin & Dev) Corpn. Ltd.	P
3.	Assam Seeds Corpn. Ltd.	M
4.	Assam State Textbook Production & Publication Corpn. Ltd.	M
5.	Assam Fisheries Dev. Corpn. Ltd.	P
6.	Assam Hills Small Industries Dev. Corpn. Ltd.	P
7.	Assam Police Housing Corpn. Ltd.	M
8.	Assam Govt. Marketing Corpn. Ltd.	P
9.	Fertichem Ltd.	M
10.	Cachar Sugar Mill Ltd. (closed)	M
11.	Assam Small Industries Dev. Corpn Ltd.	P
12.	Assam Conductors & Tubes Ltd.	M
13.	Assam Polytex Ltd.,	M
14.	Assam State Weaving & Mfg. Co. Ltd.	M
15.	Assam Electronics Dev. Corpn. Ltd.	M
16.	Assam Spun Silk Mills Ltd. (closed)	M
17.	Assam Syntex Ltd. (closed)	M
18.	Assam Tea Corpn Ltd. (privatized)	M
19.	Assam State Textile Corpn. Ltd.	M
20.	Assam Industrial Dev. Corpn. Ltd.	M

21.	Assam Petrochemical Ltd.	M
22.	Assam Gas Co. Ltd.	M
23.	Assam State Fertilizer & Chemicals Ltd.	M
24.	Ashok Paper Mill (Assam) Ltd.	M
25.	Assam Tanneries Ltd.	M
26.	Assam State Minor Irrigation Dev. Corpn. Ltd.	M
27.	Assam Mineral Development Corpn. Ltd.	M
28.	Assam Govt. Construction Corpn. Ltd.	M
29.	Assam Plantation Corp Dev. Corpn. Ltd.	M
30.	Assam Tourism Development Corpn. Ltd	P
31.	Assam Livestock & Poultry Dev. Corpn. Ltd.	P
32.	Assam Plains Tribes Dev. Corpn. Ltd.	W
33.	Assam State Dev. Corpn. for S.C. Ltd.	W
34.	Assam State Dev. Corpn. For OBC Ltd.	W
35.	Assam Minorities Dev. & Finance Corp. Ltd.	W
36.	Assam State Electricity Board	U
37.	Assam State Transport Corpn.	U
38.	Assam Financial Corpn. Ltd.	F
39.	Assam State Warehousing Corpn.	T&S
40.	Assam Urban Water Supply & Sewerage Board	U
41.	Assam Khadi & Village Industries Board	P
42.	Assam State Housing Board	M
43.	Nagaon Co-operative Sugar Mills Ltd.	M
44.	Assam Co-operative Jute Mills Ltd.	M
45.	Assam Co-Operative Sugar Mills Ltd	M
46.	Swahid Kushal Konwar Samabay	P
47.	Assam Polyester Co-Op. Society Ltd	M
48.	STATFED	M
49.	Assam Co-op. Spinning Mills Ltd. (closed)	M
50.	Assam Apex Weavers & Artisans Coop. Fed. Ltd.	M

Bihar

1	Bihar State Water Development Corp. Ltd.	P
2	Bihar State Diary Corporation Ltd.	M
3	Bihar Hill Area Lift Irrigation Corp.	P
4	Bihar State Agro Industries Dev. Corp. Ltd.	M
5	Bihar Rajya Beej Nigam Ltd.	M
6	Bihar Fruits and Vegetables Dev. Corp. Ltd.	M
7	Bihar Insecticides Ltd.	M
8	Bihar Rajya Matsya Vikas Nigam Ltd.	M
9	Bihar State Small Industries Corp. Ltd.	P
10	Bihar State Industrial Dev. Corp. Ltd.	F
11	Bihar State Leather Industries Dev. Corp. Ltd.	M
12	Bihar Scooters Ltd.	M
13	Bihar Paper Mills Ltd.	M
14	Bihar State Finished Leather Corp. Ltd.	M
15	Bihar State Glazed Tiles and Ceramic Industries Ltd.	M
16	Vishwamithra Paper Industries Ltd.	M
17	Jhanjharpur Paper Industries Ltd.	M
18	Bihar State Tannin Extracts Ltd.	M
19	Bihar Solvent and Chemicals Ltd.	M
20	Synthetic Resins (Eastern) Ltd.	M
21	Magadha Minerals Ltd.	M
22	Bhawani Active Carbon Ltd.	M
23	Kumardhubi Metal Casting and Engineering Ltd.	M
24	Bihar State Electronics Development Corp.	M
25	Beltron Video System Ltd .	M
26	Beltron Mining Systems	M
27	Beltron Informatics Ltd.	M
28	Bihar State Textiles Corp. Ltd.	M
29	Bihar State Handloom and Handicrafts Corp. Ltd.	P

30	Bihar State Forest Development Corp. Ltd.	P
31	Bihar State Mineral Development Corp. Ltd.	P
32	Bihar Police Building Construction Corp. Ltd.	M
*33	Bihar State Construction Corp. Ltd.	M
34	Bihar Rajya Pul Nirman Nigam Ltd.	M
35	Bihar State Minorities Finance Corp. Ltd.	W
36	Bihar State Backward Classes Finance and Dev. Corp. Ltd.	W
37	Bihar State Food and Civil Supplies Ltd.	T&S
38	Bihar State Sugar Corp. Ltd.	M
39	Bihar State Cement Corp. Ltd.	M
40	Bihar State Tourism Dev. Corp. Ltd.	P
41	Bihar State Pharmaceuticals and Chemicals Dev. Corp. Ltd.	M
42	Bihar Maize Products Ltd.	M
43	Bihar Drugs and Chemicals Ltd.	M
44	Bihar State Hydro Electric Power Corp. Ltd.	U
45	Tenughat Vidyut Nigam Ltd.	U
46	Bihar Panchayat Raj Fianancial Corp. Ltd.	F
47	Bihar State Warehousing Corp.	T&S
48	Bihar State Credit and Investment Corp. Ltd	F
49	Bihar State Exports Corp. Ltd.	P
50	Bihar State Text Book Publishing Corp. Ltd.	M
51	Bihar State Film Dev. Finance Corp.Ltd.	P
52	Bihar State Electricity Board.	U
53	Bihar State Road Transport Corp.	U
54	Bihar State Financial Corp.	F

Delhi

1.	Delhi State Industrial Development Corporation Ltd.	F
2.	Delhi State Civil Supplies Corporation Ltd.	P
3.	Delhi Scheduled Caste Financial & Development Corporation Ltd.	W
4.	Delhi Financial Corporation	F

5.	Delhi State Mineral Development Corporation Limited	M
6.	Delhi Tourism & Transportation Devp. Corpn. Ltd.	P
7.	Pragati Power Corporation Limited	U
8.	Delhi Power Generation Company	U
9.	Delhi Power Supply Company Limited	U
10.	Delhi Electricity Distribution Co. Ltd. (Central-East)	U
11.	Delhi Electricity Distribution Co. Ltd. (South-West)	U

Goa

1.	The Goa State Cooperative Bank Ltd.	F
2.	The Madgaum Urban Cooperative Bank Ltd.	F
3.	Goa State Horticulture Corpn. Ltd.	P
4.	Goa Housing Board	M
5.	Goa Antibiotics & Pharmaceuticals Ltd.	M
6.	Goa Tourism Development Corporation	P
7.	Kadamba Transport Corporation Ltd.,	U
8.	Goa Industrial Development Corporation	F
9.	Goa Forest Development Corporation Ltd.	M
10.	Sewage & Infrastructural Development Corporation Ltd.	S
11.	Goa Electricals Limited	M
12.	Goa State Infrastructure Development Corporation Ltd.	M
13.	Info Tech Corporation of Goa Limited	M
14.	Goa Handicrafts Rural & Small Scale Industries Development	P
15.	Goa Tourism Development Corporation Ltd.	P
16.	Goa Meat Complex Ltd.,	M
17.	Economic Development Corporation of Goa, Daman & Diu Ltd.	P
18.	Goa Auto Accessories Ltd.(Subsidiary of EDC-Goa)	M
19.	Goa State S.C.s & Other B.C.s Finance & Devp. Corpn. Ltd.	W

Haryana

1.	Haryana State Coop. Supply & Marketing Fed. Ltd. (HAFED)	P

2.	Haryana Forest Development Corporation Ltd.	P
3.	Haryana State Coop. Development Fed. Ltd.	P
4.	Haryana Financial Corporation Ltd.	F
5.	Haryana State Industrial Development Corporation Ltd.	F
6.	Haryana State Small Industries & Export Corporation Ltd.	P
7.	Haryana Handloom & Handicrafts Corporation Ltd.	P
8.	Haryana State Electronics Development Corporation Ltd.	M
9.	Haryana Agro Industries Corporation Ltd.	P
10.	Haryana Warehousing Corporation Ltd.	T&S
11.	Haryana Land Reclamation & Development Corporation Ltd.	P
12.	Haryana Seed Development Corporation Ltd.	M
13.	Haryana State Minor Irrigation & Tubewells Corporation Ltd.	P
14.	Haryana Tourism Corporation Ltd.	P
15.	Haryana Scheduled Castes finance and Development Corporation Ltd.	W
16.	Haryana Backward Classes & Economically Weaker Section Kalyan Nigam	W
17.	Haryana Women Development Corporation Ltd.	W
18.	Haryana Roadways Engineers Corporation Ltd.	U
19.	Haryana Police Housing Corporation Ltd.	M
20.	Haryana State Roads & Bridges Development Corporation Ltd.	M
21.	Haryana Minerals Ltd.	M
22.	Haryana State Electricity Board	U
23.	Housing Board Haryana	M
24.	Haryana Urban Development Authority	P
25.	Haryana State Agricultural Marketing Board	P
26.	Haryana State Khadi &Village Industries Board	P
27.	Haryana Rural Development Fund	F
28.	Haryana State Co-operative Handloom Weavers Apex Society Ltd.	P
29.	Haryana state Co-operative Apex Bank Ltd.	F

30.	Haryana State Federation of Consumer Co-operative Wholesale Store Ltd.	P
31.	Haryana State Industrial Coop.Fed Ltd.	P
32.	Haryana State Coop. Housing Fed. Ltd.	P
33.	Haryana State Coop. Labour & Construction Fed. Ltd.	P

Himachal Pradesh

1.	Himachal Pradesh General Industries Corporation Ltd.	M
2.	H.P. Horticultural Produce Marketing and Processing Corpn. Ltd.	P
3.	Shimla Development Authority	P
4.	H.P. State Civil Supplies Corporation Ltd.	P
5.	H.P. Khadi & Village Industries Board	P
6.	H.P. Sate Industries Development Corporation Ltd.	P
7.	Himachal Pradesh Housing Board	M
8.	H.P. Mahila Vikas Nigam	W
9.	H.P. Ex-Servicemen Corporation	W
10.	Himachal Worsted Mills Ltd.	M
11.	H.P. State Forest Corporation Ltd .	P
12.	H.P. Agro Industries Corporation	P
13.	Agro Industrial Packaging India Ltd.	M
14.	H.P. State Small Industries Export Corpn. Ltd.	M
15.	H.P. State Electronics Devp. Corpn. Ltd.	M
16.	H.P. State Handicrafts & Handloom Corporation Ltd.	P
17.	H.P. Road & Other Infrastructure Devp. Corpn. Ltd.	F
18.	H.P. Backward Classes Finance & Devp. Corpn.Ltd.	W
19.	H.P. Minorities Finance & Devp. Corpn. Ltd.	W
20.	H.P. Tourism Devp. Corpn. Ltd.	P
21.	H.P. Health Systems Corpn. Ltd.	P
22.	H.P. State Electricity Board	U
23.	H.P. Road Transport Corporation	U

24.	H.P. Financial Corporation Ltd.	F
25.	Nahan Foundry Limited	M

Jammu & Kashmir

1.	Jammu & Kashmir Industries Ltd.	F
2.	J & K Projects Construction Corporation Ltd.	M
3.	J & K State Handloom Development Corporation Ltd.	P
4.	Himalayan Wool Combers Ltd.	P
5.	Jammu & Kashmir State Financial Corporation	F
6.	Jammu & Kashmir State Forest Corporation	M
7.	Jammu & Kashmir Cements Ltd.,	M
8.	J&K State Handloom Development Corporation Ltd.	P
9.	Jammu & Kashmir Handicrafts (Sales&Exports) Corp. Ltd.	P
10.	Jammu & Kashmir Agro Industries Ltd.	M
11.	Jammu & Kashmir Minerals Limited	M
12.	Jammu & Kashmir State Cable Car Corpn. Ltd.	M
13.	Jammu & Kashmir State Women's Development Corpn.	W
14.	Jammu & Kashmir Agro Industries Devp. Corpn.	P
15.	Jammu & Kashmir State Road Transport Corpn.	U
16.	Jammu & Kashmir Small Scale Industries Devp. Corpn.	P
17.	Jammu & Kashmir SC/ ST/OC Development Corpn.	W
18.	Jammu & Kashmir Tourism Development Corpn.	P
19.	Jammu & Kashmir Horticultural Produce Marketing & Processing Corpn.	P
20.	Jammu & Kashmir State Industrial Devp. Cropn.	M
21.	Jammu & Kashmir Power Development Corpn.	U

Karnataka

1.	Karnataka Power Transmission Corp. Ltd.	U
2.	Karnataka State Road Transport Corp.	U
3.	North East Karnataka State Road Transport Corp.	U
4.	Karnataka Power Corp. Ltd.	U

5.	Karnataka SC /ST Development Corp.	W
6.	Karnataka Sate Financial Corp.	F
7.	Karnataka State Industrial Investment & Dev. Corp.	F
8.	Karnataka Backward Classes Development Corp.	W
9.	Karnataka State Police Housing Corp.	M
10.	Karnataka State Minorities Dev. Corp.	W
11.	Karnataka State Women's Dev. Corp.	W
12.	Karnataka State Handicrafts Dev. Corpn.	W
13.	Karnataka Agro Industries Corp. Ltd.	M
14.	Karnataka Film Industries Dev. Corp.	P
15.	Karnataka Fisheries Dev. Corp.	P
16.	Karnataka Forest Dev. Corp.	M
17.	Karnataka Compost Dev. Corp. Ltd.	M
18.	Karnataka Handloom Dev. Corp. Ltd.	P
19.	Karnataka Leather Dev. Corp. Ltd.	P
20.	Karnataka State Electronics Dev. Corp. Ltd.	M
21.	Karnataka Cashew Dev. Corp. Ltd.	M
22.	Karnataka Inland Fisheries Dev. Corp. Ltd.	P
23.	Karnataka State Coir Dev. Corp. Ltd.	M
24.	Karnataka Housing board	M
25.	Karnataka State Warehousing Corp.	T&S
26.	Karnataka State Small Industries Dev. Corp.	P
27.	Shree Kanteerava Studios Ltd.	M
28.	Karnataka State Construction Corp. Ltd.	M
29.	Karnataka State Tourism Dev. Corp. Ltd.	U
30.	Karnataka State Food and Civil Supplies Corp. Ltd.	M
31.	Karnataka Land Army Corp. Ltd.	P
32.	Jungles and Lodges and Resorts Ltd.	P
33.	D. Devraj URs Truck Terminals Ltd.	T&S
34.	Bangalore Water Supplies and Sewerage Board	U
35.	Karnataka Urban Infra Development Corp. Ltd.	M

36.	Krishna Bhagya Jala Nigam Ltd.	P
37.	Karnataka Neeravri Nigam Ltd.	P
38.	Bangalore Mass Rapid Transit Ltd.	U
39.	Karnataka Renewable Energy Dev. Corp. Ltd.	U
40.	Karnataka Road Dev. Corp. Ltd.	U
41.	Mysore Sugar Co. Ltd.	M
42.	Mysore Paper Mills Ltd.	M
43.	Mysore Lamps Ltd.	M
44.	Mysore Tobacco Co. Ltd.	M
45.	Mysore Paints Varnish Ltd.	M
46.	Mysore Match Co. Ltd.	M
47.	Mysore Chrome Tanning Co. Ltd.	M
48.	Mysore Electrical Industries Ltd.	M
49.	Hutti Gold Mines.	M
50.	NGEF Ltd.	P
51.	NGEF (Hubli)	P
52.	Mysore Acetate and Chemicals Co. Ltd.	M
53.	Mysore Cosmetics	M
54.	Mysore Minerals	M
55.	Karnataka State Agro Corn Products Ltd.	M
56.	Karnataka State Forest Industries Corp. Ltd.	P
57.	Karnataka State Veeners Ltd.	M
58.	Chamundi Machine Tools	M
59.	Karnataka Implements & Machine Co. Ltd.	M
60.	Karnataka Argo Protiens Ltd.	M
61.	Karnataka Vidyuth Karnatakakhane Ltd.	U
62.	Karnataka Silk Industries Corp Ltd.	P
63.	Karnataka Soaps And Detergents Ltd.	M
64.	Karnataka Dairy Development Corp Ltd.	P
65.	Karnataka State Textiles Ltd.	M
66.	Karnataka Telecom Ltd.	M

67.	Karnataka Pulp Wood Ltd.	M
68.	Karnataka Tungsten Molly Ltd.	M
69.	Karnataka State Powerloom Development Corp Ltd.	U
70.	Vidhya Nagar Steel Ltd.	M
71.	Mysore Sales International Ltd.	M
72.	Marketing Consultants And Agencies Ltd.	P
73.	Karnataka State Seeds Corp Ltd.	M
74.	Karnataka Meat and Poultry Marketing Corp.	M
75.	Karnataka Silk Marketing Board Ltd.	P
76.	Karnataka small Industries Marketing Corp.	P
77.	Karnataka State Khadi & Villages Industries Board.	P
78.	Karnataka State Agricultural Produce Procession & Export.	M
79.	Bangalore Metropolitan-Transport Corporation	U

Kerala

1.	The Plantation Corporation of Kerala Limited	M
2.	The State Farming Corporation of Kerala Limited	M
3.	The Rehabilitation Plantations Limited	M
4.	Oil Palm India Limited	M
5.	The Kerala Agro -Industries Corporation Limited	M
6.	The Kerala State Coir Corporation Limited	M
7.	The Kerala State Cashew Development Corporation Limited	M
8.	Kerala Agro-Machinery Corporation Limited	M
9.	Foam Mattings (India) Limited	M
10.	Kerala State Horticultural Products Development Corporation Limited	M
11.	Kerala Livestock Development Board Limited	M
12.	Kerala State Poultry Development Corporation Limited	M
13.	Kerala Feeds Limited	M
14.	United Electrical Industries Limited	M
15.	Traco Cable Company Limited	M

16.	Transformers and Electricals Kerala Limited	M
17.	Kerala Electrical and Allied Engineering Company Limited	M
18.	Trivandrum Rubber Works Limited (Subsidiary of SFCK)	M
19.	The Kerala Ceramics Limited	M
20.	Kerala Construction Components Limited	M
21.	Kerala Small Industries Development Corporation Limited (SIDCO)	P
22.	Kerala State Film Development Corporation Limited	P
23.	The Metal Industries Limited	P
24.	The Metropolitan Engineering Company Limited	P
25.	Steel Complex Limited (SCL) (Subsidiary of KSIDC)	P
26.	Steel Industrials Kerala Limited (SILK)	P
27.	Scooters Kerala Limited	M
28.	Kerala Automobiles Limited	M
29.	Steel and Industrial Forgings Limited (Subsidiary of SILK)	M
30.	Autokast Limited (Subsidiary of SILK)	M
31.	Kerala Hitech Industries Limited	P
32.	Keltron Counters Limited (Subsidiary of KELTRON)	M
33.	Kerala State Electronics Development Corporation Limited (KELTRON)	M
34.	Keltron Electro-Ceramics Limited (Subsidiary of KELTRON)	M
35.	Keltron Crystals Limited (Subsidiary of KELTRON)	M
36.	Keltron Component Complex Limited (Subsidiary of KELTRON)	M
37.	Keltron Magnetics Limited (Subsidiary of KELTRON)	M
38.	Keltron Resistors Limited (Subsidiary of KELTRON)	M
39.	Keltron Rectifiers Limited (Subsidiary of KELTRON)	M
40.	Astral Watches Limited (Susidiary of KSIDC)	M
41.	Trivandrum Spinning Mills Limited	M
42.	Kerala State Textile Corporation Limited	M
43.	Kerala Garments Limited (Subsidiary of KSHDC)	M

44.	Sitaram Textiles Limited	M
45.	Kerala State Handloom Development Corporation Limited (KSHDC)	M
46.	Kerala State Mineral Development Corporation Limited	M
47.	Kerala Clays and Ceramic Products Limited	M
48.	Kerala State Construction Corporation Limited	M
49.	Kerala Police Housing and Construction Corporation Limited	M
50.	Roads and Bridges Development Corporation of Kerala Limited	M
51.	The Kerala Land Development Corporation Limited	P
52.	Kerala State Development Corporation for Scheduled Castes and Scheduled Tribes Limited	W
53.	The Kerala State Backward Classes Development Corporation Limited	W
54.	Kerala State Handicapped Persons' Welfare Corporation Limited	W
55.	Kerala State Development Corporation for Christian Converts from Scheduled Castes & the Recommended Communities Limited	W
56.	Kerala Artisans' Development Corporation Limited	W
57.	Kerala State Palmyrah Products Development and Workers' Welfare Corporation Limited	U
58.	The Kerala State Civil Supplies Corporation Limited	T&S
59.	The Travancore Cements Limited	M
60.	Malabar Cements Limited	M
61.	Kerala Tourism Development Corporation Limited (KTDC)	P
62.	Tourist Resorts (Kerala) Limited (Subsidiary of KTDC)	T&S
63.	Bekal Resorts Development Corporation Limited	T&S
64.	The Travancore-Cochin Chemicals Limited	M
65.	Kerala Soaps and Oils Limited	M
66.	Kerala State Drugs and Pharmaceuticals Limited	M
67.	The Pharmaceutical Corporation (Indian Medicines) Kerala Limited	M

68.	Kerala State Detergents and Chemicals Limited	M
69.	Kerala State Salicylates and Chemicals Limited	M
70.	Travancore Titanium Products Limited	M
71.	The Kerala Minerals and Metals Limited	M
72.	The Travancore Sugars and Chemicals Limited	M
73.	Kerala State Industrial Development Corporation Limited (KSIDC)	F
74.	The Kerala State Financial Enterprises Limited	F
75.	Kerala Urban Development Finance Corporation Limited	F
76.	Kerala Transport Development Finance Corporation Limited	F
77.	Kerala Power Finance Corporation Limited	F
78.	Kerala State Industrial Products Trading Corporation Limited	T&S
79.	Kerala State Beverages (Manufacturing and Marketing) Corporation Limited	M
80.	Kerala School Teachers and Non-teaching Staff Welfare Corporation Limited	W
81.	Kerala State Women's Development Corporation Limited	W
82.	Overseas Development and Employment Promotion Consultants Limited.	P
83.	Kerala State Industrial Enterprises Limited (KSIE)	F
84.	Kerala State Maritime Development Corporation Limited	P
85.	Meat Products of India Limited	M
86.	Kerala Shipping and Inland Navigation Corporation Limited	U
87.	Kerala State Electricity Board	U
88.	Kerala State Road Transport Corporation	U
89.	Kerala Financial Corporation	F
90.	Kerala State Warehousing Corporation	T&S
91.	Kerala Industrial Infrastructure Development Corporation	P
92.	Kerala State Coconut Development Corporation Limited	P
93.	The Kerala Fisheries Corporation Limited	P

94.	Kerala Inland Fisheries Development Corporation Limited	P
95.	The Kerala Premo Pipe Factory Limited	P
96.	The Chalakudy Refractories Limited	M
97.	Kerala Special Refractories Limited	M
98.	The Kerala Asbestos Cement Pipe Factory Limited	M
99.	Kerala State Financial Enterprises Limited	F
100.	Tourist Resorts (Kerala) Limited	T&S
101.	Keltron Power Devices Limited	M
102.	Kerala Forest Development Corporation Limited	P
103.	The Travancore Sugars & Chemicals Limited	M
104.	Forest Industries (Travancore) Limited	P
105.	Kerala State Wood Industries Limited	M
106.	Travancore Plywood Industries Limited	M

Madhya Pradesh

1.	M. P. Agro Industries Development Corporation	M
2.	M. P. State Industries Development Corporation	P
3.	M. P. Export Corporation Limited.	P
4.	M. P. Laghu Udyog Nigam Ltd.	P
5.	M. P. State Electronics Development Corporation Ltd	M
6.	Optel Telecommunciations Ltd.	M
7.	M. P. State Textile Corporation Ltd.	M
8.	M. P. Hasthshilp Avam Hath kargha Vikas Nigam Ltd.	P
9.	M. P. Rajya Van Vikas Nigam Ltd.	P
10.	M. P. State Minning Corporation Ltd.	
11.	M. P. Police Housing corporation Ltd.	P
12.	M. P. Pichhda Varg Tatha Alpsandhyak Vittaavam Vikas Nigam Ltd.	W
13.	M. P. Adivasi Vitta Avam Vikas Nigam Ltd.	W
14.	M. P. State Civil Supplies Corporation Ltd.	P

15.	M. P. State Tourism Development Corporation Ltd.	P
16.	The Provident Fund Ltd.	F
17.	M. P. Urja Vikas Nigam Ltd.	U
18.	M. P. State Electricity Board	U
19.	M. P. State Road Transport Corporation	U
20.	M. P. Financial Corporation	F
21.	M. P. State Warehousing Corporation	T&S
22.	M. P. Lift Irrigation Corporation Ltd.	M
23.	M. P. State Dairy Development Corporation Ltd.	M
24.	M. P. Leather Development Corporation Ltd.	M
25.	M. P. Film Development Corporation Ltd.	P
26.	M. P. Rajya Setu Nirman Nigam Ltd.	M
27.	M. P. Panchayati Raj Vitta Avam Gramin Vikas Nigam Ltd.	W
28.	M. P. State Industrial Development Corporation Ltd.	M

Maharashtra

1.	Maharashtra Petrochemicals Corporation Ltd.	M
2.	Maharashtra state Textile Corporation Ltd.	M
3.	Devagiri Textile Mills Ltd.	M
4.	Kalmeshwar Textiles Mills Ltd.	M
5.	Godavari Garments Ltd.	M
6.	Maharashtra Land Development Corporation Ltd.	P
7.	The Maharashtra Fisheries Development Corporation	P
8.	Maharashtra Electronics Corporation Ltd.	M
9.	Forest Development Corporation of Maharashtra Ltd.	M
10.	The Maharashtra State Farming Corporation Ltd.	M
11.	Maharashtra State Financial Corporation	F
12.	Maharashtra Industrial Development Corporation	F
13.	Maharashtra State Seeds Corporation Ltd.	M
14.	Maharashtra Agro Industries Development Corporation	M
15.	Maharashtra Small Scale Industries Development Corporation	P

16.	Maharashtra Tourism Development Corporation	U
17.	Leather Industries Development Corporation of Maharashtra	U
18.	Leather Industries & Chermakar Community Devp. Corpn. of Maharashtra Ltd.	U
19.	Leather Industries Corpn. of Marthwada Ltd.	M
20.	Maharashtra Water Supply and Sewerage Board	U
21.	Kolhapur Chitranagari Mahamandal Ltd.	P
22.	Maharashtra State Mining Corporation Ltd.	M
23.	Maharashtra State Warehousing Corporation	T&S
24.	The Maharashtra State Cooperative Cotton Growers	P
25.	Maharasthra Mendhi Va Shell Vikas Mahamandal Ltd.	P
26.	Development Corporation of Vidarbha Ltd.	P
27.	Maharashtra State Handlooms Corporation Ltd.	P
28.	Maharashtra Film, Stage & Cultural Development Corporation	P
29.	MAFCO Ltd.	M
30.	Mahatma Phule Backward Class Development Corporation	W
31.	Maharashtra State Co-operative Oilseeds Grower's Federation	W
32.	Lokshahir Annabhau Sathe Development Corporation Ltd.	W
33.	Maharashtra Rajya Sahakari Audyogik Vasahat Federation	W
34.	The Maharashtra State Cooperative Bank Ltd.	F
35.	Parbhani Krishi Gosamvardhan Ltd.	P
36.	Vasantrao Naik Vimukta Jatis & Nomadic Tribes Development	W
37.	Maharashtra Cooperative Devp. Corpn. Ltd.	P
38.	Maharashtra State Powerlooms Corpn. Ltd.	P
39.	Pulgoan Cotton Mills Ltd.	M
40.	Maharashtra State Police Housing & Welfare Corpn. Ltd.	W
41.	Maharashtra State Road Devp .Corpn. Ltd.	U
42.	City & Industrial Devp.Corpn. of Maharashtra Ltd.	P
43.	Shivshahi Punarvasan Prakalp Ltd.	W
44.	Development Corporation of Kokan Ltd.	P

45.	Marthwada Development Corpn. Ltd.	P
46.	Western Maharashtra Devp. Corpn. Ltd.	P
47.	Maharashtra Rajya Itar Magas Vargiya Vitta Anivikas Mahamandal Ltd.	P
48.	Anna Saheb Patil Arthik Magas Vikas Mahamandal Ltd.	W
49.	Shabri Adivasi Vitta Vikas Mahamandal Ltd.	W
50.	Haffkine bio-pharmaceuticals Ltd.	M
51.	Haffkine Ajanta Pharmaceuticals Ltd.	M
52.	Krupanadhi Limited	M
53.	Mahila Arthik Vikas Mahamandal Ltd.	W
54.	Maharashtra Electricity Board	U
55.	Maharashtra State Road Transport Corpn.	U
56.	Dairy Development Corporation of Marthwada Limited	M
57.	Ellora Milk Products Ltd.	M
58.	Irrigation Devp. Corpn. of Maharashtra Ltd.	M
59.	Konkan Seafoods Ltd.	M
60.	Prabhani Krishi Gosamvardhan Ltd.	P
61.	Vidhraba Quality Seeds Ltd.	M
62.	Abhijit Samayadarshika Ltd.	M
63.	Kinwat Roofing Tiles Ltd.	M
64.	Marthwada Ceramics Complex Ltd.	M
65.	Shahyadri Glass Works Ltd.	M
66.	Gondwana Paints & Minerals Ltd.	M
67.	Vidharba Tanneries Ltd.	M
68.	Meltron Instrumentation Ltd.	M
69.	Textile Corporation of Marthwada Ltd.	M
70.	Pratap Spinning, Weaving & Manufacturing Co. Ltd.	M
71.	Maharashtra State Housing Corpn. Ltd.	M
72.	Maharashtra State Rural Development Corpn.	P
73.	The Overseas Employment & Export Promotion Corpn. of Maharashtra Ltd.	P

Manipur

1. Manipur Agro-Industries Corporation Ltd. M
2. Manipur Industrial Development Corporation Ltd. F

Meghalaya

1. Meghalaya Industrial Development Corporation Ltd. F
2. Meghalaya Tourism Development Corporation Ltd. P
3. Meghalaya Handloom and Handicrafts Development Corporation P
4. Meghalaya Mineral Development Corporation Ltd. P
5. Meghalaya Bamboo Chips Ltd. M
6. Mawmluh Cherra Cements Ltd. M
7. Meghalaya Apex Handloom Weavers & Handicrafts Cooperative P
8. Meghalaya State Warehousing Corporation T&S
9. Meghalaya Government Construction Corporation Ltd. M
10. Meghalaya State Cooperative Marketing & Consumers P
11. Meghalaya Watches Ltd. M
12. Meghalaya Electronic Development Corp. M
13. Forest Dev. Corp. of Meghalaya Ltd. P

Mizoram

1. Mizoram Food And Allied Industries Corporation Ltd. M
2. Mizoram State Cooperative Fruit Forestry and Vegetable M
3. Mizoram Electronics Development Corporation Limited M
4. Mizoram Industrial Development Corporation Ltd. F
5. Mizoram Handloom & Handicraft Development Corpn. Ltd. U
6. Mizoram Agricultural Marketing Devp. Corpn. Ltd. P

Nagaland

1. Nagaland Industrial Development Corporation Ltd. F
2. Nagaland Industrial and Raw Material Supply Corpn. M

3.	Nagaland Handloom & Handicrafts Devp. Corpn. Ltd.	P
4.	Nagaland Sugar Mills Co. Ltd.	M
5.	Nagaland Hotels Ltd.	P
6.	Nagaland Mineral Development Corpn.	M

Tripura

1.	Tripura Horticulture Corpn. Ltd.	M
2.	Tripura Forest Development & Plantation Corpn.Ltd.	P
3.	Tripura Small Industries Corpn. Ltd.	P
4.	Tripura Industrial Devp. Corpn. Ltd.	F
5.	Tripura Handloom & Handicrafts Devp. Corpn. Ltd.	P
6.	Tripura Jute Mills Ltd.	M
7.	Tripura Tea Development Corpn. Ltd.	M
8.	Tripura Rehabilitation Plantation Corpn. Ltd.	M
9.	Tripura Road Transport Corpn.	U

Pondicherry

1.	Pondicherry Agro Service and Industries Corpn. Ltd.	M
2.	Pondicherry Agro Products, Food and Civil Supplies Corpn. Ltd.	M
3.	Pondicherry Distilleries Ltd.	M
4.	Pondicherry Industrial Promotion Devleopment and Investment Corpn. Ltd.	F
5.	Pondicherry Electronics Limited	M
6.	Pondicherry Textile Corpn. Ltd.	M
7.	Pondicherry Adi-dravidar Devp. Corpn. Ltd.	W
8.	Pondicherry Corporation for Development of Women & Handicapped Persons Ltd.	W
9.	Pondicherry Backward Classes & Minorities Devp. Corpn. Ltd.	W
10.	Pondicherry Tourism & Transport Devp. Corpn. Ltd.	P
11.	Pondicherry Power Corporation Limited	U

Orissa

1.	Orissa State Ware Housing Corporation	T&S
2.	Orissa Industrial Infrastructure Dev. Corporation	F
3.	Orissa State Financial Corporation	F
4.	Orissa State Road Transport Corporation	U
5.	Orissa Mining Corporation	M
6.	Industrial Promotion & Investment Corpn. of Orissa Ltd.	F
7.	Grid Corporation of Orissa Limited	U
8.	Orissa Hydro Power Corporation	U
9.	Orissa Power Generation Corporation	U
10.	Orissa Rural Housing & Development Corporation	M
11.	Orissa Small Industries Corporation	P
12.	Orissa Lift Irrigation Corporation	U
13.	Orrisa Cashew Development Corporation	P
14.	Orissa Agro Industries Corporation Ltd.	M
15.	Agricultural Promotion & Investment Corporation of Orissa Ltd.	M
16.	Orissa Pisciculture Development Corporation	P
17.	Orissa State Seeds Corporation	M
18.	Orissa Forest Development Corporation	M
19.	Orissa Film Development Corporation	P
20.	Orissa Civil Supplies Corporation Ltd.	U
21.	Orissa Bridge & Construction Corporation	M
22.	Orissa Construction Corporation Ltd.	M
23.	Orissa Police Housing & Welfare Corporation	M
24.	Orissa Tourism Development Corporation	P
25.	Orissa State Electronics Development Corporation	M
26.	Konark Television Ltd.	M
27.	Orissa State Handloom Development Corporation	P
28.	Orissa State Leather Corporation	M

29.	Orissa Textile Corporation Ltd. (BTM)	M
30.	Orissa Textiles Mills (OTM)	M
31.	New Mayurbhanj Textiles (NMT)	M
32.	Orissa Instrument Company	M
33.	Orissa State Commercial Transport Corporation	U
34.	Orissa State Export Development Corporation	P
35.	Orissa State Beverages Corporation	M

Punjab

1.	Punjab Poultry Development Corporation Limited	P
2.	Punjab Land Development and Reclamâtion Corporation Limited	P
3.	Punjab Agro Industries Corporation Limited	M
4.	Punjab State Tubewell Corporation Limited	M
5.	Punjab State Seeds Corporation Limited	M
6.	Punjab State Container and Warehousing Corporation Ltd.	T&S
7.	Punjab State Civil Supplies Corporation Limited	T&S
8.	Punjab Small Industries and Export Corporation Limited	T&S
9.	Punjab State Industrial Development Corporation Limited	F
10.	Punjab Recorders Limited	M
11.	Punjab Renewable Energy Development and Power Generation Company Ltd.	P
12.	Punjab State Electronics Development and Production Corporation Ltd.	M
13.	Punjab Digital Industrial Systems Limited	M
14.	Consumer Electronics (Punjab) Limited	M
15.	Electronic Systems Punjab Limited	M
16.	Punjab Communications Limited	M
17.	Punjab State Forest Development Corporation Limited	P
18.	Punjab Tourism Development Corporation Limited	T&S
19.	Punjab Police Housing Corporation Limited	M

20.	Punjab State Bus Stand Management Company Limited	P
21.	Punjab State Electricity Board	U
22.	PEPSU Road Transport Corporation	U
23.	Punjab Scheduled Castes Land Development and Finance Corporation	W
24.	Punjab Financial Corporation	F
25.	Punjab State Warehousing Corporation	T&S
26.	Punjab Dairy Development Corporation Limited	M
27.	Punjab Micro Nutrients Limited	M
28.	Punjab Agro News Prints Limited	M
29.	Punjab Footwears Limited	M
30.	Punjab Tanneries Limited	M
31.	Punjab Tyres Limited	M
32.	Punjab State Leather Development Corporation Limited	M
33.	Punjab Power Products Limited	U
34.	Punjab Power Packs Limited	U
35.	Punjab Bio Medical Equipments Limited	M
36.	Punjab Electro Optics Systems Limited	M
37.	Intermagnetic India Limited	M
38.	Zimag India Limited	M
39.	PCL Telecom Limited	M
40.	Punjab Housing Finance Corporation Limited	M
41.	Punjab State Hosiery and Knitwear Development Corporation Limited	M
42.	Nakodar Cotton Waste Spinning Mills Limited	M
43.	Punjab Processors Limited	M
44.	Ludhiana Worsted Spinning Mills Limited	M
45.	Sangrur Worsted Spinning Mills Limited	M
46.	Polytex Processors Limited	M
47.	Doaba Shoddy Spinning Mills Limited	M
48.	Doaba Worsted Spinning Mills Limited	M

49.	Sutlej Shoddy Spinners Limited	M
50.	Punjab State Handloom and Textiles Development Corporation Limited	U
51.	Reliance Hotels Limited	P
52.	Punjab Film and News Corporation Limited	P
53.	Punjab Export Corporation Limited	M

Rajasthan

1.	Rajasthan State Bridge & Construction Corporation	M
2.	Rajasthan State Mineral Development Corporation Ltd.	M
3.	Rajasthan State Seeds Corporation Ltd.	M
4.	Rajasthan Electronics Ltd.	M
5.	The Rajasthan Small Industries Corporation Ltd.	M
6.	Rajasthan State Hotels Corporation Ltd.	T&S
7.	Rajasthan Tribal Areas Development Cooperative Federation	W
8.	Govt. Salt Works Didwana	M
9.	Rajasthan State Mines & Minerals Ltd.	M
10.	Rajasthan State Industrial Development and Investment Corp.	F
11.	Rajasthan Paryatan Vikas Nigam Ltd.	S
12.	Rajasthan State Agro Industries Corporation Ltd.	M
13.	Govt. Salt Works Pachpadra	M
14.	Crude Sodium Sulphate Works Didwana	M
15.	Rajasthan State Warehousing Corporation	T&S
16.	Rajasthan Land Development Corporation	P
17.	Rajasthan Financial Corporation	F
18.	Rajasthan Scheduled Caste Development Cooperative	W
19.	Rajasthan State Handloom Devp. Corpn.	P
20.	Rajasthan State Tungston Devp. Corpn.	M
21.	Rajasthan State Agriculture Marketing Board	P
22.	Rajasthan State Transport Corporation	U
23.	Rajasthan Jal Vikas Nigam	P

24.	Rajasthan State Electricity Board	U
25.	Rajasthan Housing Board	P
26.	Rajasthan State Ganganagar Sugar Mills Ltd.	M

Sikkim

1.	Sikkim Jewels Limited	M
2.	State Bank of Sikkim	F
3.	Sikkim Time Corporation (SITCO)	M
4.	Sikkim State Co-operative Supply & Marketing Federation Ltd.	P
5.	Sikkim Industrial Development & Investment Corporation Ltd.	F
6.	State Trading Corporation of Sikkim	M
7.	Sikkim Schedule Caste, Schedule Tribe and Other Backward Classes	W
8.	Development Corporation Limited	P
9.	Sikkim Mining Corporation	M
10.	Temi Tea Estate (Sikkim Tea Board)	M

Tamil Nadu

1.	T. N. Agro Industries Corporation	M
2.	T. N. Forest Plantation Corporation	P
3.	T. N. Tea Plantation Corporation	M
4.	T. N. Medicinal Plant Farms & Herbal Medicine Corpn.	M
5.	Arasu Rubber Corporation	M
6.	T. N. State Construction Corpn.	M
7.	T. N. Adi Dravidar Housing & Devp. Corpn.	W
8.	T. N. Police Housing Corporation	M
9.	State Industries Promotion Corporation of T. N.	P
10.	T. N. Power Finance & Infrastructure Dev. Corpn.	F
11.	T. N. Industrial Investment Corporation	F
12.	T. N. Industrial Development Corporation	F
13.	T. N. Urban Finance & Infrastructure Dev. Corporation	F

14.	T. N. Transport Development Finance Corporation	F
15.	T. N. Small Industries Development Corporation	P
16.	T. N. Textiles Corporation	M
17.	T. N. Handloom Development Corporation	P
18.	T. N. Film Devp.Corpn.	P
19.	T. N. Tourism Development Corpn.	P
20.	T. N. Handicrafts Devleopment Corporation	P
21.	T. N. Fisheries Development Corpn.	P
22.	Tamil Nadu Backward Classes Economic Dev. Corpn.	W
23.	T. N. Corporation for Development of Women	W
24.	T. N. Small Industries Corporation	P
25.	T. N. Sugar Corporation	M
26.	T. N. Salt Corporation	M
27.	Electronic Corporation of T. N.	M
28.	T. N. Zari Limited	M
29.	Southern Structurals Limited	M
30.	T. N. Cements Limited	M
31.	T. N. News Print and Papers Limited	M
32.	T. N. Minerals Limited	M
33.	T. N. Magnesites Limited	M
34.	T. N. Warehousing Corporation	P
35.	Overseas Manpower Corporation	P
36.	Pallavan Transport Consultancy Services	U
37.	T. N. Ex-Servicemen's Corporation	W
38.	T. N. Medical Services Corporation	P
39.	Poompuhar Shipping Corporation	T&S
40.	T. N. Civil Supplies Corporation	T&S
41.	T. N. State Marketing Corporation	T&S
42.	Metropolitan Transport Corporation	U
43.	State Express Transport Corporation-I	U

44.	State Express Transport Corporation-II	U
45.	T. N. State Transport Corporation-Villipuram Div. I	U
46.	T. N. State Transport Corporation-Villipuram Div. II	U
47.	T. N. State Transport Corporation-Villipuram Div. III	U
48.	T. N. State Transport Corporation-Kumbakonam Div. I	U
49.	T. N. State Transport Corporation-Kumbakonam Div. II	U
50.	T. N. State Transport Corporation-Kumbakonam Div. III	U
51.	T. N. State Transport Corporation-Kumbakonam Div. IV	U
52.	T. N. State Transport Corporation-Salem Div. I	U
53.	T. N. State Transport Corporation-Salem Div. II	U
54.	T. N. State Transport Corporation-Coimbatore Div. I	U
55.	T. N. State Transport Corporation-Coimbatore Div. II	U
56.	T. N. State Transport Corporation-Madurai Div. I	U
57.	T. N. State Transport Corporation-Madurai Div. II	U
58.	T. N. State Transport Corporation-Madurai Div. III	U
59.	T. N. State Transport Corporation-Madurai Div. IV	U
60.	T. N. State Transport Corporation-Madurai Div. V	U

Uttar Pradesh

1.	U. P. Nalkoop Nigam Ltd.	P
2.	U. P. State Yard Company Ltd.	S
3.	U. P. Bhutpurva Sainik Kalyan Nigam Ltd.	W
4.	The Pradeshiya Industrial & Investment Corporation	F
5.	U. P. (PASCHIM) Ganna Beej Evam Vikas Nigam Ltd.	M
6.	U. P. Hill Electronics Corporation Ltd.	M
7.	U. P. Small Industries Corporation Ltd.	P
8.	U. P. Seeds and Tarai Development Corporation Ltd.	M
9.	U. P. Bhumi Sudhar Nigam Ltd.	P
10.	U. P. State Tourism Development Corporation Ltd.	P
11.	Kumaon Mandal Vikas Nigam Ltd.	P
12.	The Uttar Pradesh State Cement Corporation Ltd.	M

13.	Uttar Pradesh Samaj Kalyan Nirman Nigam Ltd.	P
14.	U. P. Scheduled Castes Finance & Development Corporation	W
15.	U. P. Waqf Vikas Nigam Ltd.	W
16.	U. P. Pichhari Jati Vitta Evam Vikas Nigam Ltd.	W
17.	U. P. (ROHELKHAD-TARAI) Ganna Beej Evam vikas Nigam	M
18.	U. P. State Mineral Development Corporation Ltd.	P
19.	The Indian Turpentine & Rosin Co. Ltd.	M
20.	U. P. Electronics Corporation Ltd.	M
21.	U. P. Development Systems Corporation Ltd.	M
22.	U. P. State Warehousing Corporation	T&S
23.	U. P. State Food & Essential Commodities Corporation	S
24.	U. P. Police Avas Nigam Ltd.	W
25.	Uttar Pradesh Pashudhan Udyog Nigam Ltd.	P

Uttaranchal

1.	Uttaranchal Power Corporation	U
2.	Uttaranchal Jal Vidhyut Nigam	U
3.	SC/ ST Finance Development Corporation	W
4.	Uttaranchal State Industrial Corporation	F
5.	Gadwal Mandal Development Corporation	P
6.	Forest Development Corporation	P

West Bengal

1.	West Bengal State Seed Corporation Limited	M
2.	West Bengal Tea Development Corporation	M
3.	West Bengal Plywood and Allied Products Limited	M
4.	West Bengal Agro Industries Corporation Limited	M
5.	West Bengal State Minor Irrigation Corporation Limited	M
	West Bengal State Food Processing and Horticulture Development Corporation Limited	M
6.	West Bengal Dairy and Poultry Development Corporation Limited	M

7.	The State Fisheries Development Corporation Limited	P
8.	West Bengal Fisheries Corporation Limited	P
9.	Pulver Ash Projects Limited	M
10.	IPP Limited	M
11.	Krishna Silicate and Glass Limited	M
12.	West Bengal Ceramic Development Corporation Limited	M
13.	Greater Calcutta Gas Supply Corporation Limited	M
14.	West Bengal Small Industries Development Corporation Limited	P
15.	West Bengal State Leather Industries Development Corporation Limited	M
16.	Neo-Pipes and Tubes Company Limited	M
17.	Britannia Engineering Limited	M
18.	National Iron and Steel Company Limited	M
19.	The Carter Pooler Engineering Company Limited	M
20.	The Shalimar Works Limited	M
21.	The Electro Medical and Allied Industries Limited	M
22.	Westing House Saxby Farmer Limited	M
23.	Angel India Machines and Tools Limited	M
24.	West Bengal Electronics Industry Development Corporation Limited	M
25.	Webel Electronic Communication Systems Limited (subsidiary of WBEIDC Limited)	M
26.	Webel Crystals Limited (subsidiary of WBEIDC Limited)	M
27.	Webel Power Electronics Limited (subsidiary of WBEIDC Limited)	M
28.	Webel Mediatronics Limited (subsidiary of WBEIDC Limited)	M
29.	Webel Informatics Limited (subsidiary of WBEIDC Limited)	M
30.	Webel Multimedia Limited (subsidiary of WBEIDC Limited)	M
31.	Webel Consumer Electronics Limited (subsidiary of WBEIDC Limited)	M
32.	Webel Capacitors Limited (subsidiary of WBEIDC Limited)	M

33.	The Kalyani Spinning Mills Limited	M
34.	Mayurakshi Cotton Mills (1990) Limited	M
35.	West Bengal Agro-Textiles Corporation Limited	M
36.	The West Dinajpur Spinning Mills Limited	M
37.	West Bengal Handloom and Powerloom Development Corporation Limited	P
38.	West Bengal Handicraft Development Corporation Limited (subsidiary of WBSIC Limited)	U
39.	West Bengal Forest Development Corporation Limited	P
40.	West Bengal Mineral Development and Trading Corporation Limited	P
41.	The West Bengal Projects Limited (subsidiary of WBSIDC Limited)	M
42.	West Bengal Housing Infrastructure Development Corporation Limited	M
43.	West Bengal Women Development Undertaking	W
44.	West Bengal Essential Commodities Supply Corporation Limited	T&S
45.	West Bengal Sugar Industries Development Corporation Limited	M
46.	West Bengal Tourism Development Corporation Limited	P
47.	Durgapur Chemicals Limited	M
48.	West Bengal Pharmaceutical and Phytochemical Development Corporation Limited	M
49.	Eastern Distilleries and Chemicals Limited	M
50.	West Bengal Chemical Industries Limited	M
51.	The Infusions (India) Ltd.	M
52.	Gluconate Health Limited	M
53.	The Durgapur Projects Limited	M
54.	The West Bengal Power Development Corporation Limited	U
55.	West Bengal Rural Energy Development Corporation Limited	U
56.	The West Bengal Industrial Development Corporation Limited	F

58.	West Bengal Infrastructure Development Finance Corporation Limited	F
59.	The Calcutta Tramways Company(1978) Limited	U
60.	West Bengal Surface Transport Corporation Limited	U
61.	West Bengal Transport Infrastructure Development Corporation Limited	U
62.	Silpabarta Printing Press Limited (subsidiary of WBSIC Limited)	M
63.	West Bengal Film Development Corporation Limited	U
64.	Basumati Corporation Limited	M
65.	Saraswaty Press Limited	M
66.	West Bengal State Electricity Board	P
67.	West Bengal Electricity Regulatory Commission	P
68.	Calcutta State Transport Corporation	P
69.	North Bengal State Transport Corporation	P
70.	South Bengal State Transport Corporation	U
71.	West Bengal Financial Corporation	U
72.	West Bengal Industrial Infrastructure Development Corporation	F
73.	West Bengal Scheduled Castes & Scheduled Tribes and Backward Classes Development & Finance Corporation	W
74.	West Bengal Minorities Development & Finance Corporation	W
75.	Great Eastern Hotel Authority	U
76.	West Bengal State Warehousing Corporation	T&S
77.	The West Bengal Livestock Processing Development Corporation Limited	M
78.	Webel Video Devices Limited (subsidiary of WBEIDC Limited)	M
79.	Webel Carbon and Metal Film Resistors Limited (subsidiary of WBEIDC Limited)	M
80.	West Bengal Wasteland Development Corporation Limited	P
81.	Sundarban Sugarbeet Processing Company Limited	M
82.	Lime Light Industries (Private) Limited (subsidiary of WBSIC Limited)	M

Table-1: Total Investment

State/Year	1990-91	1991-92	1992-93	1993-94	1994-95	1995-96	1996-97	1997-98	1998-99
Andhra Pradesh	26,741.83	33,507.62	40,159.69	62,453.25	63,996.63	74,571.83	81,065.53	90,243.36	102,125.04
Arunachal Pradesh	29.54	32.23	39.05	38.28	47.73	44.75	50.72	42.35	35.18
Assam	2,261.98	2,576.69	2,826.94	3,052.35	3,280.68	3,490.25	3,670.21	3,819.06	762.27
Delhi	5,330.28	6,171.49	6,583.36	7,658.34	8,901.18	9,773.58	9,291.26	10,933.54	12,915.30
Goa	139.61	178.42	203.42	246.74	328.24	400.65	475.84	756.64	919.11
Gujarat	7,671.30	8,840.61	9,927.32	11,301.25	12,737.49	14,667.54	16,582.92	19471.58	15958.06
Haryana	543.7	623.76	718.87	773.81	920.11	1,064.28	1,287.83	1,589.76	870.26
Himachal Pradesh	983.59	1,057.15	1,102.17	1,133.24	1,419.60	1,545.81	1,740.25	1,963.66	2,230.67
Jammu & Kashmir	258.24	279.52	307.48	337.78	382.49	442.42	497.04	1188.03	1392.18
Karnataka	8,616.57	9,369.77	10,593.71	11,974.33	13,727.10	17,207.70	18,638.18	15454.3	20380.528
Kerala	5,135.12	14,840.92	5,067.15	4,360.20	8,157.20	6,242.58	9,670.29	9600.79	9832.2
Madhya Pradesh	499.88	546.3	620.35	657.43	685.62	814.65	808.82	762.8	811.2
Maharashtra	13,040.83	15,154.35	19,658.46	27,878.62	34,592.10	38,697.04	49,021.96	60,448.47	19,958.05
Manipur	56.11	58.85	64.17	113.82	122.13	127.32	128.77	134.48	140.73
Meghalaya	396.28	443.66	467.06	485.04	498.89	528.38	535.76	616.05	504.89
Mizoram	404.2	394.42	504.82	516.02	517.3	502.17	561.66	1,170.51	0.55
Nagaland	79.77	80.97	88.29	91.48	90.08	97.99	173.21	181.24	187.07
Orissa	7,095.20	7,727.85	8,238.31	8,592.40	9,099.23	8,078.87	10,647.15	11,491.40	13,370.25
Pondicherry (U.T.)	48.31	88.41	100.07	116.08	142.39	163.21	197.1	256.3	324.17
Punjab	7,776.51	8,388.87	9,293.51	10,204.51	11,711.14	13,024.07	13,424.40	15,428.96	5,315.78
Rajasthan	3,148.85	3,594.40	4,234.97	5,016.81	6,117.18	6,711.20	7,519.28	2739.49	2903.44
Uttar Pradesh	10,867.97	12,384.16	14,171.11	15,119.29	16,311.09	16,990.90	18,576.59	20535.04	3516.37
Total (state wise)	105,933.27	131,836.67	140,486.76	178,526.43	201,574.27	226,738.14	253,695.68	279,497.61	220,842.49

Table-2: Capital Employed

Rs.in Crores

STATE / YEAR	1990-91	1991-92	1992-93	1993-94	1994-95	1995-96	1996-97	1997-98	1998-99
Andhra Pradesh	3,743.89	7,679.54	9,374.92	11,036.17	13,678.40	14,915.55	14,446.63	16,532.79	19,410.66
Arunachal Pradesh	24.41	26.82	33.89	50.73	52.04	73.52	89.35	38.62	33.59
Assam	1,985.09	2,284.06	2,510.49	2,678.60	2,883.25	3,059.02	3,204.75	3,350.73	391.9
Delhi	7,219.67	9,422.51	10,731.63	10,161.74	9,195.75	11,048.33	12,481.89	12,873.23	12,279.58
Goa	136.5	178.43	206.62	229.95	332.64	389.6	460.93	948.15	947.2
Gujarat	6,500.86	7,325.26	7,979.17	8,598.51	9,821.87	11,226.21	12,744.56	30645.09	34475.04
Haryana	1,254.42	1,400.94	1,650.94	1,884.28	2,267.78	2,600.79	831.25	1,117.25	974.59
Himachal Pradesh	984.51	1,070.13	1,148.99	1,177.42	1,365.36	1,510.64	1,660.18	1,850.41	2,054.42
Jammu & Kashmir	401.16	408.76	365.82	302.07	270.59	259.89	291.78	309.53	308.32
Karnataka	8,487.57	9,208.06	10,380.81	14,245.73	12,727.89	15,992.81	17,488.08	15054.66	20251.22
Kerala	2,805.26	3,002.96	5,094.05	3,676.56	4,869.98	4,989.00	6,085.37	6878.1	9280.67
Madhya Pradesh	534.21	567.39	3,572.90	4,792.62	6,910.37	11,067.72	11,086.16	9,227.08	6,833.87
Maharashtra	7,889.28	8,341.47	10,705.53	19,497.21	23,739.71	31,092.46	37,200.21	44,934.52	6,711.99
Manipur	38.66	112.79	41.07	40.51	41.26	42.62	19.21	18.2	19.33
Meghalaya	343.35	368.47	402.15	33,952.29	434.21	458.87	456.07	444.29	446.5
Mizoram	229.18	258.12	296.17	315.43	345.53	381.39	411.73	421.39	332.02
Nagaland	-112.42	-136.43	-155.12	-175.77	-285.65	-41.17	11.85	8.67	0.4
Orissa	1,207.20	1,051.30	914.95	796.17	622.57	3,287.07	5,766.24	5,961.21	6,639.35
Pondicherry (U.T.)	53.66	118.2	130.97	165.37	181.17	189.13	197.22	236.48	266.68
Punjab	7,299.89	7,736.88	8,787.15	9,928.64	11,559.35	12,523.08	12,857.11	15,345.81	3,616.72
Rajasthan	4,182.49	4,772.69	5,485.80	6,489.00	8,039.55	9,224.36	10,478.65	3963.89	4445.53
Sikkim	30.83	44.5	49.91	49.03	41.92	43	37.38	39.3	18.48
Tamil Nadu	5,712.31	6,693.32	7,188.11	8,300.90	10,059.28	11,854.60	13,073.72	13,965.24	10,576.29
Tripura	36.11	59.95	61.88	62.12	52.67	59.62	70.4	79.85	40.33
Uttar Pradesh	8,144.32	[illegible],598.72	9,406.83	12,109.11	14,924.72	15,643.16	17,208.14	18251.74	~
Total (state wise)	69,132.41	80,594.85	96,365.63	150,364.39	134,132.21	161,891.25	178,658.85	202,496.23	140,354.68

Table-3: All States : Net Worth

Rs.in Crores

State/Year	1990-91	1991-92	1992-93	1993-94	1994-95	1995-96	1996-97	1997-98	1998-99
Andhra Pradesh	1,601.94	1,870.59	2,179.29	3,204.01	8,646.81	5,063.20	6,548.01	7,197.53	7,939.90
Arunachal Pradesh	**7.78**	**9.84**	**12.18**	**14.72**	**22.03**	**27.86**	**21.79**	24.24	17.03
Assam	**-528.24**	**65.17**	**33.23**	**30.78**	**-85.94**	-222.71	**-577.31**	**-938.69**	**33.99**
Delhi	2,629.30	2,628.29	2,789.60	3,515.83	5,274.12	6,446.59	4,243.47	4,910.71	5,046.16
Goa	62.57	89.84	110.18	126.2	230.57	278.36	315.66	681.58	473.61
Gujarat	959.68	1,161.06	1,428.48	1,699.43	2,101.46	2,517.83	2,998.59	3,050.73	8308.85
Haryana	826.26	911.14	1,099.36	1,358.81	1,574.44	1,820.44	507.54	605.54	477.25
Himachal Pradesh	736.11	803.62	842	892.34	1,202.71	1,353.78	1,573.78	1,776.14	1,974.82
Jammu & Kashmir	85.52	22.47	-38.63	-116.75	-8,873.45	-278.18	-341.04	833.17	898.79
Karnataka	2,272.30	2,445.17	2,809.07	3,432.90	3,366.83	4,920.78	5,527.06	6,017.83	6,806.15
Kerala	496.09	391.42	-502.01	320.68	667.82	822.96	990.96	1,301.03	2.35
Madhya Pradesh	146.46	159.16	144.21	148.05	128.86	91.12	98.68	107.56	109.82
Maharashtra	3,991.88	5,713.08	5,646.21	4,724.15	5,081.62	5,386.76	5,752.94	10,270.08	5,254.80
Manipur	9.67	0.07	14.57	57.74	52.27	43.17	36.94	34.91	33.75
Meghalaya	324.91	357.67	386.54	416.17	424.45	450.07	444.55	422	434.53
Mizoram	**413.61**	**407.16**	**521.41**	**538.35**	**540.67**	**540.2**	**585.96**	**1,215.46**	~
Nagaland	**188.12**	**210.46**	**233.02**	**254.34**	**367.17**	**119.22**	**139.83**	**146.82**	**159.74**
Orissa	-4,180.88	-4,421.59	-4,744.87	-5,032.96	-5,769.88	-1,817.42	-1,470.01	-2,077.47	-3,071.70
Podicherry (U.T.)	30.32	76.56	85.87	87.18	105.39	112.47	123.82	182.37	84.43
Punjab	1,228.71	1,228.83	2,966.66	3,091.19	3,348.61	3,657.22	4,643.71	4,565.85	-244.93
Rajasthan	**-231.24**	**519.05**	**654.15**	**844.67**	**982.56**	**1,542.70**	**1,935.10**	**2,896.48**	~
Sikkim	**23.7**	**23.22**	**23.68**	**20.95**	**13.25**	**16.49**	**15.47**	**16.86**	**-0.11**
Tamil Nadu	1,180.76	1,573.78	1,140.03	1,637.49	2,255.40	2,308.95	3,184.51	3,538.40	3,312.60
Tripura	36.85	43.1	48.87	52.95	51.75	60.18	67.12	75.25	36.85
Uttar Pradesh	**-37.11**	**58.46**	**112.47**	**-42.13**	**83.43**	**-62.28**	**-277.29**	**-300.66**	~
Total (state wise)	12,275.07	16,347.65	17,995.57	21,277.10	21,792.95	35,199.77	37,089.85	46,553.72	28,785.02

Table-4: All States : Total Revenue Earned

Rs.in Crores

State/Year	1990-91	1991-92	1992-93	1993-94	1994-95	1995-96	1996-97	1997-98	1998-99
Andhra Pradesh	4167.54	4914.15	11157.52	6584.66	7,659.39	11035.68	10491.93	14469.34	14997.51
Arunachal Pradesh	19.45	18.89	25.07	29.28	31.02	27.35	36.33	21.65	11.67
Assam	541.22	568.08	584.2	626.36	693.64	1046.05	887.68	837.72	165.54
Delhi	11037.97	12063.77	13391.09	12790.62	13710.66	20571.44	4118.63	5185.92	4986.05
Goa	31.5	38.75	55.29	63.19	93.03	98.66	99.77	119.91	384.91
Gujarat	3657.73	4401.09	4759.77	5452.99	6216.77	7645.72	8911.47	9651.59	1732.01
Haryana	620.18	845.26	822.86	862.89	922.95	1071.92	895.12	976.29	732.25
Himachal Pradesh	301.55	328.46	379.29	415.35	491.2	568.65	683.54	809.96	916.62
Jammu & Kashmir	115.35	100.42	132.28	134.21	145.65	195.38	232.47	311.06	406.02
Karnataka	7396.97	8856.31	10830.31	10801.08	11241.85	13864.4	16127.22	16047.03	14342.88
Kerala	1680.6	2,884.70	2430.58	2533.26	2888.29	4727.25	3820.37	4941.3	5320.31
Madhya Pradesh	542.1	655.14	786.51	833.1	880.78	1018.66	1246.78	386.91	371.7
Maharashtra	2857.5	3138.18	4139.59	4551.53	5261.6	5902.97	6346.24	8283.14	5870.83
Manipur	8.58	10.61	10.9	8.61	13.03	9.68	8.34	7.79	6.43
Meghalaya	59.61	74.94	77.74	101.11	96.52	117.28	134.16	154.34	127.75
Mizoram	160.19	165.17	181.58	210.13	208.33	199.7	256.16	319.13	10.34
Nagaland	-53.92	-77.16	-99.32	-120.79	-232.94	-57.62	0.19	-1.14	-7.61
Orissa	4825.07	5832.09	4830.86	6356.06	6932.19	7182.99	7421.5	7,292.77	6,123.69
Pondicherry (U.T.)	17.23	115.19	133.24	153.01	174.28	174.69	177.16	163.23	135.68
Punjab	3776.68	4313.61	5261.48	6692.75	7859.18	9165.96	9604.01	10706.54	3738.23
Rajasthan	1302.3	1806.85	2347.83	2821.26	3374.28	4201.64	4778.45	5611.18	1770.13
Sikkim	21.35	30.66	27.19	26.13	24.83	36.05	43.45	41.99	22.79
Tamil Nadu	5213.92	6043.36	7250.11	6968.88	9778.77	11466.46	13365.35	14420.94	6299.38
Tripura	12.35	14.17	12.51	13.69	10.51	12.82	14.9	15.95	13.28
Uttar Pradesh	**4275.62**	**5073.34**	**5988.74**	**6895.87**	**7697.35**	**8844.27**	**9351.77**	**10733.25**	~
Total (state wise)	52,588.64	62,216.03	75517.22	75805.23	86173.16	109128.05	99,052.99	111,507.79	68,478.39

Table-5: All States : Net Profit

Rs.in Crores

State/Year	1990-91	1991-92	1992-93	1993-94	1994-95	1995-96	1996-97	1997-98	1998-99
Andhra Pradesh	-105.22	-275.65	-223.57	41.53	1,562.34	-113.85	-99.66	235.24	140.52
Arunachal Pradesh	**-0.03**	**1.1**	**2**	**1.88**	**7.28**	**3.85**	**3.59**	**-0.96**	**~**
Assam	**-136.72**	**-268.22**	**-216.35**	**-311.16**	**-459.85**	**-243.08**	**-686.18**	**-643.47**	**-27.93**
Delhi	94.73	-150.44	328.03	19.22	225.84	307.15	444.02	480.63	256.36
Goa	0.69	1.43	2.08	-0.71	9.41	-4.08	-4.77	1.53	-2.05
Gujarat	134.88	100.94	176.05	154.62	173.44	261.61	294.65	119.78	163.18
Haryana	20.36	1.72	-0.27	2.82	7.73	-6.81	8.68	101.32	-742.87
Himachal Pradesh	1.91	-0.5	7.75	13.33	21.45	43.14	60.78	83.05	-7.6
Jammu & Kashmir	-12.52	-60.22	-45.21	-64.59	-51.49	-73.03	-42.4	-69.49	-68.55
Karnataka	63.73	96.44	-43.24	-22.85	23.87	53.47	130.76	571.31	286.39
Kerala	-144.74	-4,203.77	-132.29	-64.26	-2.63	0.33	-93.25	-119.04	0.42
Madhya Pradesh	14.16	14.11	47.55	28.76	19.51	8.15	20.64	-5.72	-4.93
Maharashtra	11.3	99.6	7.33	57.81	92.45	100.14	-101.43	-35.04	-273.89
Manipur	-2.55	-1.74	-2.38	-4.81	-4.95	-7.6	-6.9	-9.11	-7.59
Meghalaya	-11.06	-41.48	-25.07	-46.62	-11.56	-14.92	-12.97	-11.69	-34.99
Mizoram	-377.65	-474.33	-543.35	-501.93	-550.47	-628.82	-639.87	-570.96	-35.62
Nagaland	-8.33	-10.11	-9.08	-7.02	-81.33	246.7	-17.42	-4.57	-9.55
Orissa	-314.11	-458.54	-539.97	-304.71	-815.98	-695.81	-827.75	-1,378.51	-1,423.93
Pondicherry (U.T.)	1.32	4.52	1.56	-7.23	-7.23	-18.56	-25.64	-17.6	-15.44
Punjab	-18.24	-43.26	-75.72	162.68	-241.48	25.7	-11.73	77.39	-157.83
Rajasthan	**-93.9**	**81.12**	**72.19**	**111.77**	**99.01**	**241.39**	**131.53**	**97.96**	**~**
Sikkim	**1.37**	**1.89**	**0.73**	**-0.65**	**-7.38**	**-3.12**	**-0.15**	**2.48**	**-6.81**
Tamil Nadu	60.56	283.98	239.93	281.88	368.12	230.02	71.2	54.39	-506.97
Tripura	-8.51	-9.73	-10.23	-11.93	-13.46	-13.93	-15.24	-17.67	0.82
Uttar Pradesh	**-173.72**	**23.58**	**134.88**	**-190.03**	**83.05**	**-214.28**	**-681.06**	**-344.2**	**~**
Total (state wise)	-1,002.28	-5,287.57	-846.65	-662.21	445.68	-516.23	-2,100.56	-1,378.74	-2,691.10

2

Modalities of PE's Reforms and Privatisation of SLPEs*

State level public enterprises (SLPEs) produce a variety of products and provide a gamut of services. They vary in size, capital intensity, product, age, performance and profitability. Therefore the strategies for reforming these would also vary. The issues in categorising them and the nature of the reforms and their modalities are presented in this paper.

PART-I

Actions proposed for the reform of SLPEs

As SLPEs vary in terms of products and performance they are first to be categorized in order to determine the nature and scope of the reforms to be implemented in respect of each.

As many Public Enterprises have been formed with a view to provide a public purpose to mobilize resources from non Government sources and to provide revenue surplus to the state, these public enterprises may be categorized with reference to the following three dimensions

* T.L.Sankar, R.K.Mishra and R.Nandagopal, SLPE Working group, Institute of Public Enterprise, Osmania University Campus, Hyderabad-500 007

1. Public Purpose
2. Resource mobilization
3. Profitability

By placing them on the three dimensional they will therefore fall into 2x2x2 i.e. 8 categories as follows:

Category 1: Public purpose high, resource mobilization high, profitability, SLPEs this category should be continued since they are good performers, they should be releved from government control. Memorandum of Understanding (MoU) should specify support to be produced and financial returns expected by the Government. The company should be made autonomous and as well as it should follow the financial obligations to the Government.

Category 2: Public performance low, resource mobilization low, profitability low. a fit case for liquidation of total disvesture if possible. This would lead to avoidance of further investment thereby reducing the burden on the exchequer.

Category 3: Public purpose high, resource mobilization low, and profitability low. To be continued in the state sector but first the accent of resource mobilization and profitability should be increase toward this end. Partial privatization could be attempted.

Category 4: public purpose high, resource mobilization low, profitability high. This could be continued in the state sector and partial privatization and increased borrowings on commercial terms could also be sort to improve mobilization.

Category 5: Public purpose high, resource mobilization high, profitability low. While this could be continued in the state sector there should be total reorganization and internal management to profitability.

Category 6: Public purpose low, resource mobilization high, profitability low. Such cases should go in for disinvestment. Total disvestiture should also be attempted.

Category 7: Public purpose low, resource mobilization low,

Profitability high. In such cases the government fund could be withdrawn by borrowing more from the market and institutions and view of the good profitability. Fit case for partial disvestiture and leading to full disvestiture.

Category 8: Public profit low, resource mobilization high, profitability high. These appropriate cases for total disinvestment which lead to capital accretions to state government.

Reorganization for internal management to improve efficiency

In case where accounting systems are still government oriented commercial actions should be adopted a clear definition of corporate mission and objectives and short term goals which have to be specified. MoU should be signed between the companies and the government.

- Internal environment could be improved through OPTIMA which stands for Optimum Performance Thorough Internal Management Action. This could be done by the changes in structure, strategy, systems and sale s based on unit wise diagnostics.
- Partial divestiture could be affected by public floatation, licensing, contracting and resorting to availing of the leased services. Appropriate steps to be taken in the case of each company should be decided on the basis of the nature of the market, market environment, profitability of the investment and perceptions about the future management. Buyouts are appropriate for companies with low capital intensity, low public purpose or where the performance in respect of resource mobilization or profitability are not very relevant. Leasing out and contracting could be resorted to in parts of a enterprise whose performance could become a specific cause center and whose production is in a highly competitive market.

Pre conditions for privatization

For adopting privatization wholly or partially the corporation should follow certain legal, accounting , financial and socio-economic pre-condition and requirements. These should be properly examined and finalized before implementing privatization proposals. The methods for divestiture depend on the existing state of the capital market. The profitability of the enterprise, the competitiveness of its products and the proporting of the total equity that is divested.

The methods of divestiture would vary form sale by auction in the enterprise as a whole through tenders or by flotation of the equity in the stock market partially.

Modalities

The success of partial or total privatization could depend on the modalities adopted. The modalities adopted should lead to objective selection of the persons or institutions who share the ownership, the most equitable compensation for the equity to be disinvested and the transparency. The adoption of the modalities should be with a view to get the best price for the government while ensuring that the company would be managed well in future.

PART-II

Need and urgency of reforms of SLPEs in India

The wave of reforms and restructuring is sweeping the entire Indian economy. SLPEs, being an important component of the public enterprise system in the country cannot escape the winds of change. These enterprises are characterized by heavy investments, very low productivity and chronic loss making. The state governments owning and managing these enterprises are facing a severe resource crunch. The eighth plan is based on the premise that the state government will play a major role in the economic development of the country. Many centrally sponsored state schemes are being transferred to the state governments and it is proposed that unless otherwise warranted the central government will not take up afresh such schemes for the state governments. The state governments are under pressure for taking up many measures to improve institutional equity and to provide more efficient social services. This implies that the financial resources of the state governments will be under constant pressure to match the demands place on them by the recent changes in the economic policy. It is natural that under the existing circumstances and the state government needs to have a fresh assessment of their policy with regard to the investments in the new and existing SLPEs. There is need also to improve the performance of existing SLPEs stretching from strategic management reforms to their total privatizations.

Analysis of current status and classification of SLPEs

SLPEs do not from a homogenous group of similar enterprises. Their performance, their market position, their public purpose vary widely. IPE on the basis of its studies of public enterprises (PE) in India and abroad is suggesting the following classification of central public enterprises under three dimensions:

a. Public purpose or social objectives.

b. Market position monopoly and competitive.

c. Financial performance, profitable or non-profitable

In the case of SLPEs there are hardly any which have monopoly market structure except in the utilities sector like electricity board or water supply. We are therefore proposing a three dimensional matrix for SLPEs which substitutes resource mobilization in place of market conditions. Many SLPEs were set up in 1970's with the sole objective of enabling the state government department to mobilize money from national and international financing agencies.

Bases on the information available which admitted is not complete a very tentative classification of industries has been made from this with reference to public purpose, extent of resources etc.,

Categorisation of SLPEs			*No. of*	*Suggested Action*	*Anticipated Results*
Public Purpose	*Resource mobilisation*	*Profitability*	*SLPEs*		
H1	H2	H3	25	Continue in the state sector with greater autonomy	Better service to consumers
L1	L2	L3	200	Closure or Liquidation or total divestiture	Saving of Govt Resources
H2	L2	L3	360	Continue in the state sector with increased accent on resource mobilisation and profitability	Improved fulfilment of public purpose
H1	L2	H3	75	Increased accent on the resource mobilisation / partial disinvestment	Better Revenues or reduced budget support
H1	H2	L3	50	Disinvest	Additional resource to Govt.
L1	H2	H3	55	Introduce financial adjustments and then of in for disinvestment	Long term Improvement in service to consumers
L1	L2	H3	49	Introduce financial adjustments and then go in for disinvestment	Long term Investment in service to consumers
L1	H2	L3	-	Disinvest	Reduced Govt. support

a. The public purpose served by the SLPE

b. The extent of resources mobilized from outside the state budget by the SLPE

c. The financial profitability of the SLPE

Based on these three major factors, we can develop a three dimensional matrix showing high and low for the three components separately

This analysis has been done purely with a view to arrive at the number of enterprises to be treated in different ways. One the whole, the number of SLPEs to be retained in public sector might be around 500 in all the states, while about 250 come for different methods of restructuring. In effect, most of the manufacturing enterprises among SLPEs qualify for immediate disinvestment. A few of them are doing well financially. A close examination shows that in some cases the preferential purchase facilities afforded by the government departments and monopoly rights over raw materials etc., give them a financial advantage, as a first step, the manufacturing enterprises in the state sector might have to be given very careful scrutiny including those SLPEs who are financially well run. These SLPEs which are to be retained in the public sector will require infusion of large funds for revitalisation. The disinvestment of financially successful manufacturing enterprises can provide funds for them.

It will be noticed that both in respect of enterprises, which have, low public purpose but also low profitability as well as high profitability as well as high profitability, disinvestment suggested to government should be nil and this would lead to avoidance of fresh investment to the government as such would improve the states fiscal situation. Different states with different fiscal backgrounds will have to adopt this.

Basis for recommendations to continue category 1 enterprise

These enterprises have a high public purpose, high rate of resource mobilisation and adequate financial viability. A case in point could be the NGEF and the Southern Structurals in the manufacturing sector. Many of IPE studies indicate while the financial performance is adequate there are not entrepreneurial and as fast growing as in the private sector with the same financial performance. This is due to the restrictions imposed by the government controls and the need for getting government clarifications for many decisions such as diversification and modernisation. It is therefore suggested that such companies should be subjected to cold privatisation i.e. they should be treated almost like private enterprise with only one senior representative from the government to keep an eye on the working on its board for evolving of strategic decisions of the enterprises. A memorandum of understanding (MOU) should be drafted. In respect of these enterprises companies some high financial targets should be set and it should be left to the enterprises to work out the details.

Basic for recommending enterprises to be continued in the state sector but with reorganisation of internal management

(Categories 3,4 and 5)

The categories of enterprises which fall under this are those with high public purpose but with low profitability. IPE study indicated that many SLPEs have been set up especially in the non-industrial sector like promotional, trading, welfare without even the basic procedures of accounting or marketing and personnel management. They will first have to understand that they have to become commercial and not be considered as par tof the department.

They will have to introduce commercial accounting substitute for the government accounting and set up commercial performance objectives. The setting up of commercial performance objective will imply an excess income over expanses. To distance the enterprises will have to be incorporated as public corporations or government companies. The incorporation in such form will arm these enterprises with power to formulate their own recruitment, purchase, and hire and fire policies as separate entities distinct form the government. These enterprises will transact business on their own and they will have to look only in such circumstances to the governments under when situations are beyond control. The first step will be to define the corporate mission and objectives of each enterprise. The conflict between the social and political contents of the objectives will have to be resolved and their relative importance will have to be made clear. As a prelude to defining objective, the mission constituting the central purpose of various enterprises will have to be laid down in a very clear-cut manner. The financial and non-financial targets will sprout form the objectives. The interface relationship, between the state government and the enterprises will have to be made transparent. The expectations of the state government form these enterprises in respect of investment decisions, raising of financial resources declaration of dividends, appointments to various posts will have to be made concise and clear. MOU cam be a good instrument to ensure accountability of the SLPEs to the government, on the one hand and obligations of the state governments to the SLPEs on the other hand. The MOU has been introduced as a performance evaluation system in the case of 140 central PEs. The MOU exercise in the case of the central PEs shows that it specifies the mission, objectives and goals of enterprises, their physical targets for particular financial year, the assumptions on which targets are based the obligations which are expected to be fulfilled by the central government and the weights assigned to the various performance targets. The enterprises are then graded as per their performance.

A tested method for improvement of internal environment in SLPEs is OPTIMA which stands for "Optimum Performance through Internal Management Action". This will entail changes in structure, strategy, systems and styles in the management of the SLPEs. Coming to structure, it can be said that many of SLPE have been following the mechanistic style of managing organisations, as they continue to remain confused about choosing among functional, product and matrix organisation structures. It is difficult to understand as to why the state diary development corporations or state electronics development corporations should continue to have function-based structure instead of opting out for the product-based or matrix structure. Interestingly, the present organisation structures in the SLPEs do not provide answers to questions about the adequacy of the managerial personnel let alone their capability skills. The SLPEs will have to evolve strategies based on the bottom-up approach, on the one hand, ad the management by objective on the other. The nature of pricing policy to be followed will have to be made transparent in this stage. The efficiency improvements sought will have to be also delineated. Another important components of strategy are performance. The SLPEs will have to clearly lay down financial targets and other performance targets. The questions as to how performance is to be monitored who will undertake this task on an ongoing basis will also have to be tackled as a part of strategy. The performance is affected by fiats issued by the controlling authorities.

The restructuring package will have to center around systems. The accounting, management information and personnel and remuneration systems will have to be X-rayed. The preparation and finalisation of accounts has remained a difficult task for the SLPEs. While developing accounting systems the question as to whether the accounting systems, particularly the accounting manual and costing systems are appropriate for a commercial enterprise will have to be attended to. The role of the management information will have to be attended to the role of the management information will have to be intensively studied. The task such as the identification of the information requirements for efficient management and systems requiring to provide timely information will have to be attended to. The development of system will include the installation of suitable sub-systems to support the requirements relating to recruitment, retention, development and motivation of staff in these enterprises. The systems in respect of remuneration will look into questions as to what terms and conditions of employment are required to secure form and retain and motivate employed of the necessary caliber in the SLPEs. The development of systems, in fact, will have to follow the board-based approach of internal audit which suggests not only the installation of systems in the different functional fields of management but also takes stock of the efficiency of such system. Thus the business management systems such as strategic planning corporate planning, production planning and control, marketing information and research, and inventory controls systems, etc. will have to be not only installed but their smooth operations will also have to be ensured.

Basic for the recommendation regarding partial disinvestment

This relates to enterprises with high public purpose but with low resource mobilisation and high profitability or high resource mobilisation or low profitability. In such case the structure of public purpose demands that the state presence would be required but other aspects of performance could be improve inducting private enterprises through partial disinvestment.

The partial divestment means diluting the hold of the state governments on theses enterprises in respect of ownership, management and financing. This partial divestment can be effected by off-loading the share capital in the SLPEs to the extent of 49 per cent. The Companies Act, 1956, defines a government company as a company in which the state has 51 per cent of more shareholding. The arguments given in support of such partial divestment is to gain resources without losing such a partial divestment. An important advantage accruing form this will be bringing market touch resulting into competitive edge to these enterprises. The partial divestment in respect of management function can take form such as inducting private parties to take over recruitment, management information system, internal audit, strategic planning and internal transport activities for the SLPEs. The partial divestment of financing in the SLPEs may mean approaching the capital market for both the equity and long term debts and resorting for short term finance through the money market instruments. In view of the lack of availability of funds on competitive conditions in the capital market as also the ambitious plans many such enterprises have relating to expansion, it is highly desirable that they make forays in the capital market. The rules governing the mobilisation of fixed deposits entitle the SLPEs to mope up money for their working capital and medium-term financing requirement. It is strange that many SLPEs have not exploited this important source. The partial divestment can be a mid-way between the wholesale bureaucratisation and complete privatisation of the SLPEs.

Modalities of Privatisation

a. **Public flotation** : Public floatation is the public offering of shares based on a prospectus. The floated company is listed and its shares are quoted on the stock exchange. Public flotation reaches the widest range of private investors and institutions. However, it demands the most meticulous preparation and marketing of the issues. The state governments will have to prepare prospectuses to provide essential information to potential shareholders, and to market the offer vigorously they will have to ensure that it reaches all interested parties. Private sales take the form of private placements with institutional investors or a group of interested parties and trade sales to other private sector companies.

b. **Private Placement** : Frequently, part of a public floatation is through private placements with institutional investors. Less often, the whole of an offer of shares is placed in this way. A private placement with interested parties may take the form of a sale to a consortium of commercial companies, one of which takes responsibility for managing the enterprise. The outcome is typically some form of joint venture.

c. **Trade Sale** : A trade sale is direct sale to corporate entity. The process may entail a negotiated sale with one potential buyer, or a tender with a number of bidders. The sale is usually based on an information memorandum which is similar in content to, but often less detailed than, a prospectus. The process is less demanding for the seller than a public flotation because the buying company is able to conduct its own investigation of the acquired business before completing the purchase.

d. **Management Buyouts**: The management buyouts are being discussed as an important alternative in the areas of the privatisation of the SLPEs. In the management buyouts the managers of the enterprise acquire control of the assets of the business. Such buyouts are invariably highly leveraged and the assets acquired are used as security to borrow a large part of the purchase price. Such buyouts can be opted out by big business houses, employees and the managers. Management Buyouts may be followed by a public flotation to enable the original buyers to realise part or all of their capital and/or to reduce gearing.

e. **Choice of Method**: We have discussed above the various methods of divestitute which method is the best for the SLPEs? No single method can be uniformly applied to the SLPEs. The choice will depend on a combination of the following factors.

   (i) the capacity and state of the capital markets;

   (ii) the attitude of the capital markets and potential shareholders to the enterprise;

   (iii) the past profitability of the enterprise and its prospects;

   (iv) the competitiveness of the market within which the enterprise operates;

   (v) the proportion of the enterprise that is to be sold.

For a public flotation to succeed, the capital market needs to be well enough developed to absorb the offer of share.

Secondly, the enterprise needs to be attractive to potential investors in terms of profitability and its continued maintenance. The state governments will do well to create conditions leading to cent-percent or subscription to such flotations by the employees, rural folk, workers etc.

It is advisable that to ease a capital market constraint on the scale of a public flotation, the immediate impact of the offer of shares can be reduced by selling the equity of the company in trenches and issuing part paid share. The balance of the issue price to be paid by the investor in one or more installments at a later date.

Trade sales are often the easiest and quickest method of divestitute. However, a number of issues should be examined prior to making an offer for sale. These may include the reasonableness of the price, concessions demanded by the bidders, impact on competitive condition in the market, attitude foreign ownership and proposed purchase of the enterprise by the existing management.

Management buyouts are emerging as an important technique of privatisation. The special features of a management buyout is the direct stake it gives to a management already knowledgeable about the enterprise and the resulting strong commitment of management to the success of the business. In case of the management buyout including employee participation, the chances of success of privatisation increase phenomenally due to an integration of employees with the privatised firm. The management buyouts reduces the need for public disclosure of confidential information and minimises the strings attached to privatisation in the form of concessions to be extended to private parties.

To be successful, the management buyouts have to be proposed by teams which can put upon attractive funding package and have intrinsic strength for effective management. They should be able to get money from the financial institutions taking advantage of the financial leverage. The business they propose to takeover should have a strong case flow and a strong asset base not needing huge capital investments in the short-term.

Preconditions for Privatisation

The decisions to privatise the SLPEs will have to be proceeded very carefully to fulfill certain pre-conditions. These can be classified a s legal, accounting, financial and socio-economic requirements necessary to be complied with prior to launching the privatisation programme.

a. **Legal Pre-conditions** : There may be several legal issues emanating from the privatisation proposal of the SLPEs. Some of them are as follows.

(i) Mode and Methods of divestiture

(ii) Employees related issues

(iii) Compliance of the provisions of statutes such as the Indian case of public offers, compliance of the requirements of the rules formulated by the stock exchanges.

(iv) Regulation of privatised enterprises in the public interest and

(v) Controlling privatised enterprises by internal mean i.e., Golden shares

As noted earlier the mode of transferring ownership of the SLPEs form the public to the private sector will depend on the type of enterprises involved. In the case of enterprises incorporated under the Companies Act, the transfer can be effected in accordance with the provisions of Companies Act in the manner similar to that employed in the transfer of private sector companies. In the private sector, the ownership is transferred from one hand to the other simply by way of sale of shares to a new company so transferred is already not listed on the stock exchange , then it is necessary to comply with the regulations of the concerned stock exchange in order to get the listing. However, the transfer of ownership in the case of the SLPEs is having a joint-venture with a private enterprise the latter may ask for the transfer of shareholdings of the former in the case of divestment. In such a case, privatisation can be preceded only if the contractual issue are first resolved. The question of mode of a statutory body which is not incorporated under the Companies Act. The transfer of ownership of such a body or part of its activities cannot be effected simply by means of transfer of shares in the body since there are no shares to be transferred. In a public corporation there are no shares and no share holders, the transfer therefore cannot be effected by way of an executive order. The only way to effect the transfer is through an enactment. For instance, under the Act the assets and liabilities in the case of an SLPE to be privatised can be transferred to the concerned administrative Ministry, which, in turn, may transfer the assets to the newly created company. The question as to whether the institutionally created company has received a fair price for its assets will get automatically resolved. The parties who have been affected by such transfer can seek the grievance redressal under the mechanism well established under the legal system. The companies so privatised will have to go in for listing at the stock exchanges for they will have to follow the same set of rules as applicable to their counterparts in the private sector. This will mean their incorporations as a public limited company, the issue of prospects for mobilising money through public subscriptions and payments of listing fees to the stock exchanges.

The privatisation may cause legal difficulties with regards to security of tenure of employees and their pension and provident fund payments. In privatising a statutory body the rights of the employees may be affected in so far as the newly set up company may not be willing to absorb all the employees on their existing terms. Any abridgment of the security will be found ultravires if challenged in court. In such instance, the best practice will be to allow the employees for the voluntary switching over to the new company. Those not willing to switch over may be absorbed into other government department. It is relevant here to refer to the Article 12 of the Indian Constitution which according to one interpretation equates public bodies as a part of the State. Thus, the employees of PEs enjoy the same rights and privileges as those enjoyed by a public servant. This will have to be taken care of.

The issue of government regulation and control of privatise enterprises is very crucial for the point of view of public interest. A good chunk of SLPEs are operating in sectors which have a great bearing on the public interest. The state electricity boards and state road transport corporations are cases in pint. Even after privatisation the state governments in such cases may like to retain control on these enterprises. Such controls can be effected by way of both external and internal measure. External controls by the state governments can be imposed by way of legislative requirements through the regulatory power boards the concerned Act may provide for setting up a Power Commission or for the road transport corporations, they may provide for setting up a road transport corporations authority. These authorities may regulate among other things the distribution of services and tariffs.

The internal controls over newly privatised enterprises can be achieved by the golden shares, the golden share arrangements one under which the government retains a special rights which may include the following.

1. Rights to withdraw in transfer of substantial shareholdings.
2. Rights in regard to appointment of Director
3. Veto rights in regard to changes in the company memorandum and articles of associations and
4. Rights concerning management decisions and business policies.

a. **Accounting Pre-conditions** : Prior to privatizing the SLPEs a number of accounting adjustments need to take place. These will include write-offs, changes in the method of accounting, preparation and finalization of accounts, and selection of valuation methods. All intensive study of the balance sheet and profit and loss account, will have to be made to ascertain that they create a favorable impression in the minds of the investor.

Once the decision to privatise is taken, the process of write-offs and readjustments should start much in advance privatisation so as to ensure that certain undesirable items do not appear in the financial statement at the time of privatisation of the SLPEs. These will include preliminary expenses, accumulated losses, capital works in progress, share application money pending issue of share capital, huge advances given by the state governments without earmarking them as equity or debt capital, bad debt reserves, etc. the preparation and finalisation of accounts and annual reports of the SLPEs should get the topmost priority. It is common place that the annual reports and accounts of a large chunk of the SLPEs are not finalized in time. The reasons assigned for this phenomenon include non-availability of vouchers, absence of primary books of accounting, lack of adequate accounting staff, and non-appointment of auditors by the Comptroller and Auditor-General of India, etc.

Some enterprises can present an improved financial showing by changing the method of accounting. It has been observed that enterprises providing financial services would pay less tax and interest on working capital if they change the method of accounting from mercantile to cash system. This may hold true even in the case of agro-industries corporation, chit-fund companies and financial enterprises run by the state governments.

b. **Socio-Economic Pre-conditions**: The formulation of any scheme of privatisation will have to take into consideration the political and social environment governing the SLPEs. The BJP, Janatadal, Congress (I), All India Anna Dravida Munnetra Kazagam led state governments have partially succeeded in their privatisation efforts due to their present political philosophy. The general disenchantment with the performance of the SLPEs in these states has not aroused public opinion against privatisation. Surprisingly, even the workers have welcomed the privatisation moves. However, in the West Bengal where the left-front government is in power, the privatisation of SLPEs have not made much headway due to a different sociopolitical environment. However, there too, a broad thinking on non-privatisation reforms is underway. In most of the states there is a general agreement to the effect that the SLPEs must reform their working least they are closed down or privatised in not too distant a future.

c. **Financial Pre-conditions**: Certain financial pre-conditions will have to be created for the privatisation of the SLPEs. These will include capital restructuring, suitable capital market conditions and extending of fiscal incentives to the general investing public to invest their money in the shareholdings of the SLPEs. The capital restructuring will result into reduction of the equity base in the SLPEs. This will enable the private sector entrepreneurs after the takeover of such enterprises to mobilize large sums by way of debt capital from the capital markets and the financial institutions. The state governments will have to popularize the stock markets in the general investing public. Almost all the states in the country excepting smaller ones now have stock exchanges and therefore listing of the issues may not be a difficult task. The state governments can take an initiative to appoint a chain of jobbers, brokers and sub-brokers who may operate from the villages and link the villages with the capital markets. The mutual funds, provident fund authorities, trusts etc., may also be lured to buy the shares of the SLPEs.

Methods of Valuation

d. **Stock Exchange Method**: This method suggests the privatisation of an enterprise based on the share price as existing on the date of privatisation. It is believed that the stock exchange prices of shares represent true worth of an enterprise. It is very simple to understand and very easy to operate. Thus, it is very easy to privatise a public enterprise based on this method. However, there may be certain objections to this method. It is said that the rumor of privatisation might result into bullish or bearish impact, on the case may be, on the share prices of an enterprise. The insider's information may result into terrific gains for some individuals. Further, this method is useful only in such cases where an enterprise is listed on stock exchange. However, some of these criticisms do not hold much ground in that instead of taking the share prices as of a particular day, an average of share prices for a specific period, say 3 months to 3 years, can be taken up to iron-out the biases.

e. **Net Tangible Assets Method**: Under this method the fair value or price of the asset of a target organisation is estimated by first computing the net chargeable assets for shares and then determining the market price of the assets in relation to the price of similar enterprises already operating in the market. The net tangible assets can be worked out by first taking the total assets figure and then subtracting from such a figure the total sum of current liabilities, long term debt, value of intangibles and losses accumulated. To this some would have to be added the value arising out of revaluation of assets. If the undertaking has to be closed down or sold out, then a sum equivalent to the value of the net tangible assets must be obtained from the investors. In case, the undertaking has a share capital base, them the net tangible assets should be divided by number of shares which will give the figure of net tangible assets per share or net assets value per share. The shareholdings can then be transferred to buyers in the terms of net assets value per share.

f. **Price Earnings Ratio Method**: The price earnings ratio can be computed from accounting records in the same way as one computes the net tangible assets ratio. The earnings per share can be calculated by estimating the normal profits after tax or by taking current actual profits after tax and then dividing earnings figures by number of outstanding shares. This number is then compared with an actual market price of an enterprise similar to the target organisation. If the price to earnings ratios of comparable enterprise are known one can convert the earnings per share of the target organisation to an estimate of fair price of that organisations's shares as price of share = P/E x EPS is going price thus calculated could be taken as a guide to decide on the value of the target value for the purpose of privatisation. The Bombay Stock Exchange Director, the

Kothari's Directory, etc., can be referred to obtain an idea of the price earnings ratio of comparable undertakings.

g. **Dividend Value Method**: According to this method the price of the share of an enterprise is the present value of the future expected dividends of the enterprise discounted at the capitalization rate appropriate for that enterprise.

This method suggests that the market price of an organisation targeted for privatisation can be found by estimating likely future dividends on the basis of the behavior of some firms in the market and by discounting the dividends cash flows by an appropriate capitalization rate. The dividends figures can be calculated first by determining the earning per share and then estimating the likely dividends based on the usual practice of the targeted organisation or on the basis of likely dividend policy.

The selection of the valuation method will have to be done by taking into consideration the specific characteristics of an SLPE and the market conditions.

Implementation of Reforms

Not only that reforms need to be conceptualized, their effective implementation is even more important. Each state may design its own elaborate implementations mechanism keeping in view its political and administrative systems. However, it is advisable that a board mechanism is followed by each state to introduce an element of transparency and objectiveness in the privatisation programme. A four-tier structure may be required for this purpose. To begin with, a committee of secretaries or a commission may be set up to look into all the cases of privatisation may make recommendations on case to case basis to the decision makers. Secondly, the rules and procedures for privatizing the SLPEs should be decided, these shall be widely publicized. Thirdly, the objectives for each case of privatisation should be formulated and privatised carefully. Finally, a time-schedule for the privatisation of each enterprise should be drawn-up and all steps be taken to implement it accordingly.

3

Divesting State Ownership – A Tale of Two Companies*

The proposal to sell equity in the enterprises owned by the Central Government is expected to bring about a change in the role and operations of public enterprises in India. It is a process through which Government hopes to change the face of the troubled economy. Like the Central Government since 1950, State Governments have also set up a large number of industrial enterprises. These State owned units are in sectors ranging from infrastructure, Agro-processing industry, mining and construction. The State Governments have also found that many of these enterprises are a drain on their finances. Badly planned, poorly managed and heavily indebted, the operations of these enterprises have been criticized by the Committees that have examined their working. A major reform in the functioning of these enterprises has to become an important component of the programme to strengthen the finances of the State governments. The sale of shares owned by the State Governments in U.P. State Cement Corporation (UPSCC) and Auto Tractors Limited (ATL) has attracted considerable interest. In case of UPSCC a petition h as been filed in the High Court against the State Government alleging that proper valuation of

* J.L. Bajaj, Adviser (Industry & Minerals), Planning Commission, New Delhi-110 001.

assets was not undertaken and that the unit was being sold at a very low price. As action in both the cases was taken at about same time, it is instructive to see why in one case there has been a strong opposition while the other process of transfer has been firmly smooth. Many State Governments are contemplating to transfer ownership of public enterprises to private entrepreneurs. Therefore, the procedure followed and the objections raised in these cases may have lessened for them.

Government of Uttar Pradesh has been running a cement factory in Chruk, since 1954. Later another factory was set up at Dalla, which went into production in 1972. The installed capacity of the two units is 4.8 lakh tones and 4 lakh tones of cement production respectively. In 1972 the ownership of these units which were being run as the departmental undertakings was transferred to the UPSCC.

The Corporation has added a linker factor with a capacity of 8 lakh tones and a unit for mixing and grinding slag at Chunar. This unit has the capacity produce 16.8 lakh tones of cement.

Table 3.1 Capacity utilization of the Three Plants Since 1981-82

Year	*Chruk*		*Dalla*		*Chunar*		*Total*	
	Production	*Capacity Utilisation*	*Production*	*Capacity Utilisation*	*Production*	*Capacity Utilisation*	*Production*	*Capacity Utilisation*
1981-82	2.87	59.8	1.20	30.0	2.69	31.98	6.76	76
1982-83	2.32	48.3	0.42	10.7	6.56	78.12	9.30	54
1983-84	2.12	44.16	0.85	21.3	6.69	116.9	9.66	66
1984-85	1.86	38.8	0.82	20.5	6.39	55.9	9.07	44
1985-86	0.05	1.06	0.50	12.44	10.34	90.40	10.89	53
1986-87	0.66	13.86	0.34	8.42	9.10	54.15	10.10	39
1987-88	0.97	20.27	0.29	7.15	10.25	60.98	10.50	14
1988-89	0.85	17.60	0.89	22.20	9.60	57.16	11.34	44
1989-90	0.11	2.47	0.08	2.05	9.00	53.57	9.20	35

The State Government has subscribed the total paid up capital of the Corporation. The paid up capital has increased from Rs. 37.08 crores in 1980-81 to Rs. 67.73 crores in 1989-90. The outstanding long-term loans given by the State Governments upto 1988-89 were Rs. 5.76 crores. In addition, the loans outstanding and interest accrued and due on loans to financial institutions as on 31.3.90 were Rs. 86 crores. In this way the total long term funds invested in the Corporation at the end of 1988-90 were Rs. 169.48 crores.

Table 3.2 Financial Position of the Company from 1986-87 to 1989-90

Sources of funds	*1986-87*	*1987-88*	*1988-89*	*1989-90*
Paid up Capital	60.00	61.53	63.53	67.73
Share Capital	10.53	2.00	4.20	0.55
Reserves & Surplus	0.05	0.05	0.05	0.05
Cumulative Profit/Losses at the end of the year	-56.81	-82.81	-124.28	-155.26
Net Worth	4.68	-19.49	-56.95	NA
Debt Equity Ratio	0.91:1	0.89:1	0.80:1	NA

Between 1981-82 – 1989-90 production of cement in Chruk declined from 2.87 lakh tones to 0.11 lakh tones; in Dalla from 1.20 lakh tones to 0.08 lakh tones but in Chunar the cement production increased from the 2.69 lakh tones to 9 lakh tones. The combined capacity utilization of the three plants declined from 76.4% in 1981-82 to 35.94% in 1989-90. As a result of indifferent operations of the plants and low capacity utilization, the cumulative losses of the Corporation reached Rs. 155.26 crores at the end of 1989-90. The reason for low capacity utilization was many. Cement manufacturing through wet process has become obsolete. As a result of poor maintenance the incidence of breakdown increased. There was little effort every to carry out routine and regular maintenance. It was reported supervisory officers that even maintenance manuals and operating manuals were not available in the plant offices.

Absence of regular maintenance along with low capability of technical personnel was responsible for frequent breakdowns in the plant. Whenever information of stoppages was collected it was not analyzed and as a result no advantage was derived from this information. The Dalla cement factory was operating at low capacity also due to inherent defects in plant design and recurring labour problems. The Chunar plant did not have the required complement of trained technical staff.

Considering the mounting losses in the operations of public enterprises, the State Government set up a committee in August, 1990 to consider various options including that of:

(i) Giving management contracts to private managers of selected enterprises while retaining State ownership.

(ii) Private entrepreneurs may found the additional capital requirements while the State Government may retain majority shareholding.

(iii) Majority shareholding to be transferred to private entrepreneurs and the State to retain minority shareholding.

(iv) Outright sale of unit.

(v) Closing down the unit and sell its assets.

Proposals were invited from private promoters for improving the viability of UPSCC. Their proposals ranged from taking over the management to purchasing machinery and other assets of the units. Seven parties responded to the State Government's invitation these were: -

The Committee held discussions with the private parties and stipulated parameters according to which proposals were invited from them. The private promoters were informed that the State Government will not provide any funds in future to the Corporation. All requirements of funds for repair, maintenance, balancing equipment or modernization will have to be arranged by the promoters. Initially, the State Government would be prepared to transfer upto 51% of its shareholding, but all future investment for expansion would have to be provided by the private promoters. The State Government would also snot stand guarantee for any transaction of UPSCC with any bank or financial institution. The State Government will, however, assist the promoters in obtaining concession or the financial institutions as are available to other stick units. The State Government will also consider deferring payment of liabilities due to Stat Government and its agencies. It may also make available sales tax determinate concession as is applicable to new industrial units. The Chairman will be the nominee of the State Government and M.D of the promoters and the representation on the Board of Directors of the Corporation will be in the same ratio of shareholding.

The Committee got the value of the shares of UPSCC assessed by M/s Billimoria & Company. Their representatives to the plants based their assessment on the audit report and audited cost sheet for 1989-92 and a brief visit. M/s Billimoria & Company carried out no physical verification and valuation of plant and machinery other than given in the Annual Report and Audited Balance Sheet. On the question of a fair price for shares, they based their report taking into account:

(i) Additional investment requirement for plant and equipment.

(ii) Future earning potential of the company.

(iii) Total assets and liabilities of UPSCC.

It was estimated that an additional investment of Rs. 56.33 crores would be required immediately to improve the operational efficiency of the three plants. The additional Disinvestment would be distributed as follows.

(i) Chruk (wet process)	Rs. 13.35 crores
(ii) Dalla (wet process)	Rs. 29 crores
(iii) Dalla (dry process)	Rs. 26.56 crores
(iv) Chunar	Rs. 10.70 crores
	Rs. 56.53 crores

The cost of creating 25.6 lakh tonne of new cement capacity at Rs. 1750 per tonne for wet process, Rs.2000 per tonne for dry process and Rs. 500 per tonne for slag grinding plant was estimated at Rs. 364 crores. The current value of the fixed assets was derived on the basis of Book Depreciation Method and Balance Useful Life Method. On Book Depreciation Method the current value of plant and machinery was assessed at Rs. 145.88 crores. After additional capital investment of Rs. 56.33 crores. It was expected that the three units would operate at 90% capacity utilization. The estimated useful life of Chruk (Wet) Dalla (Wet) and Dalla (Dry) and Chunar plants was estimated as 15 years, 25 years and 30 years respectively. The current asset value of these plants was assessed at Rs. 232.75 crores and the net asset value which was derived by deducting the value of new investments of Rs. 5653 to be made as Rs. 176.62 crores. The maximum operating capacity was to be reached after four years. Therefore, at the capacity utilization the net current value of assets was assessed at Rs. 139.82 crores. There was not much difference between the value of plants based on Balance Useful Life Method and the determination of revalued assets based on capitalization of operating profits. The former was estimated as Rs. 139.82 crores and the latter Rs. 147.07 crores. M/s Billamoria & Co., recommended the fair share value as follows:

	Rs. Lakhs
Equity	6828.21
Present Losses	16361.76
Accumulated Losses (1990-94)	2440.07
Appreciation	
Fixed Assets	8394.29
Present Value of Net Tax Savings	4892.11
Total Equity Funds	1312.78
(Dividend by number of Shares - Share Deposit of Rs. 50 lakhs converted into Shares)	6828.16
Fair Share Value	Rs. 19.23 Say Rs. 20 per Share

This assessment is based on the assumption that there would be no reduction in the strength of workers in the Corporation. The total manpower employed in the three plants was 4463. On the basis of existing norm the requirement of manpower was estimated at 3100. About 1300 excess staff i.e. about 30.6% was estimated as surplus. Inspite of low capacity utilization and surplus staff the Corporation was making much overtime payments. Also as a large number of regular workers neglected their duties and the work did employing casual labour do being got. When Chunar unit was commissioned, it was stipulated that the entire surplus staff at Dalla will be transferred first before any new labour was recruited. However, this could not be accomplished due to decision of the State Government not to shift most of the staff from Dalla. As a result of labour indiscipline, ineffective suppression, political interferences, the cement production per worker in UPSCC was sonly about .5 -. 6 tone as compared to industry norm of 2.5 - 3 tonne per worker.

The Committee treated the report of M/s Billmoria & Co. as indicative of the strength and weakness of the Corporation. They did not accept the share value as given by them as final and held further discussion with private promoters. M/s Raymond Woolens Limited conveyed their interest only in purchasing the assets. They informed that they were not interested in having a joint venture as they felt that due to high cost of the coal, power, and low productivity of labor, the operations of this unit could not be carried out on profitable basis. U.P. Asbestos Limited also did not give a credible offer. Only two promoters gave proposals that were pursued by the Committee. ACC Limited conveyed their interest in purchasing 51% shares over a period of three years. They proposed that the management of the Corporation should be transferred immediately to them. Dilemmas also offered to buy 51% of the equity. If offered they were willing to hold larger equity in the Corporation. Both Dalmias and ACC agreed to take over all the employees through both the parties felt that such a large staff was a drag on the operations of the Corporation.

The Committee asked with the promoters to convey their offers in writing. At this stage, ACC with drew their earlier offer and informed the Committee that they were no longer interested in pursuing the proposal. This left only M/s Dalmia Industries in the field. Government of U.P. and M/s Dalmia Industries then entered into a joint sector agreement in February, 1991 in respect of U.P. Cement Corporation. The important features of the agreement were:

(i) Dalmias will take over the management of UPSCCL. Taking over of the assets and liabilities of UPSCCL will be on as in where is basis.

(ii) The State Government will hold 49% of equity and Dalmias 51% in UPSCCL.

(iii) The shares with face value of RS. The State Government will transfer 100 to Dalmias and others at Rs. 75 per share.

(iv) On entering the agreement Dalmias will pay Rs. 5 crores to the State Government and the balance amount shall be paid within 24 months which will carry an interest of 12% p.a from the date of the agreement till the date it is paid to the State Government. The balance amount will be reinvested by the State Government as secured loan and will carry an interest of 12% p.a. This loan will be repaid after 5 years sin 4 equal installments.

(v) Whenever the State Government decides to disinvest the remaining shares Dalmia and its nominees will have the first right to purchase the shares at a mutually agreed price to be fixed at that time.

(vi) All employees of UPSCCL will be taken over by the joint sector venture Representation on the board of Directors will be in the same ratio as shareholding. State Government will have four Directors Dalmias. Five Directors on the Board of the Corporation. The Chairman will be nominated by the State Government out of the four Directors and the full-time Managing Director by the Dalmias out of their five nominees.

(vii) The capital base of the Corporation will not be changed without prior consultation and agreement of the State Government. The State Government will not invest any funds other than indicated earlier in UPSCCL. The State Government will also not give any guarantee for any funds to be raised in future by the management of UPSCCL. After the joint sector company comes into existence, the State Government will grant sales tax deferment facilities for five years. It will also re-sched8ule the liabilities due to the State Government and its agencies upto Rs. 25 crores. There will be a moratorium on the payment of these liabilities for three years and they will be repaid in five equal annual installments. The interest payment for these re-scheduled liabilities will be 12% with a rebate of 43% for timely and prompt payments. There will be no moratorium on interest payments. The contingent liability of Rs. 1.4 crores to sales Tax Department and Rs. 11 lakhs towards stamp duty shall be waived. The Sales Tax Department will also drop up all pending cases against UPSCCL.

(viii) If Dalmias are not able to meet any of the commitments given to the State Government at the time of formation of the joint venture, the State Government will be at liberty to take over the management of the Company.

The decision to transfer the management of the Corporation and to disinvest employees of the Corporation opposed the shareholding and they launched and agitation against take over by Dalmias. A petition was filed in the Allahabad High Court and U.P. Government was prohibited from converting UPSCC into private company. Government of U.P. Transferred 49% of equity of UPSC to M/s Dalmia Industries with the stipulation that the additional 2% will be transferred after the decision of the Court. The Government handed over the management of the UPSCC to Dalmias. But as there was labour unrest the factory premises could be transferred only with the help of the Police. The Police also had to resort to firing to control the labour who was allegedly damaging the Corporation's property. As a result of the firing 9 laborers died and production in the cement plant stopped. Since then the Court has appointed two audit firms to conduct a fresh valuation of the Corporation's property.

Table 3.3 The Production Targets, Actual Production, Sale And Cost Of Production Per Tractor/Engine Since 1981-82

		1981-82	*82-83*	*83-84*	*84-85*	*85-86*	*86-87*	*87-88*	*99-89*
Production Envisaged In the Project	T	500	2000	3500	5000	6000	6000	6000	-
report	E	-	200	1000	1500	2000	2000	2000	-
Annual	T	-	-	-	1000	500	350	450	5
Target	E	-	-	-	100	635	850	1250	200
Production	T	151	381	721	450	400	175	113	36
	E		1	11	410	600	740	285	278
Sale	T	150	281	707	396	351	361	127	12
	S	-	1	8	246	616	775	273	267
Sale Price	T	0.51	0.55	0.55	0.55	0.61	0.61	0.89	0.69
Per unit In Rs. Lakh	E			0.25	0.25	0.25	0.27	0.29	0.25
Cost per	T	1.69	1.63	1.14	1.81	2.26	2.54	3.86	8.42
Unit in Rs. Lakh	E			0.22	0.22	0.22	0.78	1.28	2.60

ATL was established in Pratapgarh, a backward district of U.P. for manufacturing tractors and diesel engines. The project liability report was prepared by HMT, which envisaged production of 7500 of 28 BHP tractors and 2005 diesel engines per year. The estimated cost of the project was Rs. 18.86 crores of which the State Government was to contribute Rs. 7.50 crores and the balance was to be given by the IDBI as term loan. The feasibility report also projected that the undertaking was likely to incur losses in the first three years of its operation, but would start earning each profits from the fourth year at 67% capacity utilization. Initially the company was to import more than 80% of components required, but was projected to achieve 100% in designation within three years of the beginning of commercial production. The company entered into a technical collaboration agreement with M/s Leyland Motors in 1979 and started manufacturing tractors from October 1981. Due to price escalation, as against the estimated cost of Rs. 18.86 crores, the actual project cost increased to Rs. 26.32 crores.

The operation of the undertaking has been facing technical and financial difficulties from its inception.

Till 1989-90, Corporation manufactured 2,380 tractors. This was less than the production target set for the first two years of its operation. As against the expectation of cash profit from fourth year of the commencement of the production, cash losses continued to mount. They were met by the State Government by advancing loans to the Corporation. Some of the factors responsible for the poor performance of the Corporation were as follows:

(i) The inappropriate choice of technology significantly the performance of corporation.

M/s Leyland who provided the technical know-how had discontinued the production of 28 BHP tractors in 1972. ATL were, therefore, in no position to incorporate in their design advances made in technology and changes in consumer preferences. By the mid 1970s tractors were being used in agricultural operations as well as for transport men and materials. The tractors manufactured by ATL were not suitable for such multipurpose use. These tractors had certain obsolete features like mechanical draft control system, low weight sheet, small size and low lifting capacity. Consumer preference, however, was for big size and heavy weight tractors. Before or after entering into the technical collaboration agreement no survey of formers' preference was made and as the collaborator had ceased manufacturing this model, market testing could not be done.

(ii) The project report made unrealistic assumptions about demand projections and the speed with which indigenization could take place. The Corporation was manufacturing only 50-55 components of the 900 parts in a tractor. The rest were being procured from various vendors. A difficulty in coordinating the procurement of parts from such a large number of sources was a complex operation. The fact that technical collaborator had ceased manufacturing the model compounded the difficulties. Components that were not available indigenously also could not be imported for this reason.

(iii) The established installed capacity of tractor manufacturing units in the country in 1989 was 1,40,000. Production of tractors increased from 85,500 in 1984-85 to about 1,70,000 in 1989 and in that year about 1,00,000 tractors were sold. The highest production achieved by ATL was 721 tractors in 1983-84 as against the annual production of 6000 envisaged in that project report. At such a level of production it was not possible for ATL to successfully compete with the already established models, provide adequate after sales service or launch successfully a credible market campaign.

(iv) As production was heavily dependent on procurement from different vendors, the location of ATL in a backward district with inadequate communication difficulties added the list of drawbacks faced by the company. Also, the demand for components being very small the suppliers did not give priority to the orders placed by ATL.

The assumption of 100% indigenization in three years was highly impractical. Even where technical collaborators actively supported the production programme, such a high level of

Table 3.4 Capital Structure, Long Term & Short Term Loans, Cumulative Cash Losses By The State Government

Rs. Lakhs	*1982-83*	*83-84*	*84-85*	*85-86*	*86-87*	*87-88*	*88-89*	*89-90*
Share Capital Contributed By the State Govt.	750.00	750.00	750.00	750.00	750.00	750.00	750.00	750.00
Loan advanced by the State Govt.	493.70	917.89	1204.78	1599.66	1986.54	2231.44	2727.33	325.4
Total investment by the State Govt.	1243.70	1667.89	1954.78	2349.66	2736.54	2981.44	3477.33	4004
Institutional Finance	807.34	975.00	1269.58	1267.53	1434.16	1648.97	1883.64	2169
Total Investment	2051.04	2642.89	3224.36	3617.19	4170.70	4630.41	5360.97	6173
Accumulated loss	583.20	928.53	1399.86	1943.80	2494.29	2999.83	3876.35	4794

indigenization has not been achieved. In this case the technical collaborator did not supply even the basic drawings and process sheets required for the development of an indigenization programme especially of proprietary items. Therefore, production continued to depend on imported components.

As against the estimated cost of 18.86 crores, the actual cost at which the project was set up was Rs. 26.32 crores which was higher by about 39% than the original estimate.

The operations of ATL have been examined by several Expert Committees. They recommended that the Corporation could not be viable by manufacturing of 28 BHP Leyland tractors and diesel engines. The State Government also examined the possibility of manufacturing three-wheeler vehicles in this plant. But considering intense competition and lack of expertise, it was decided not to venture in this field. As it became evident that it would not be possible to operate the unit profitably, it was decided in November, 1990 to close down the operations. All the employees numbering about 1230 were paid compensation and were retrenched. The State Government appointed a Committee to recommend various options regarding the disposal of the assets of ATL. The Committee appointed a firm of chartered accountants who were also auditors of ATL to value the assets. The chartered accountants assessed the value of assets at Rs. 8.8 crores. In their view if there was a change in product line, the value of plant and machinery could be even lower. The Committee invited offers from private promoters for operating the plant in joint sector. Five private promoters responded to the proposal and expressed interest in taking over the assets. They were: (i) M/s Raunaq Industries Limited, (ii) M/s Kanoria Industries Limited (iii) M/s P. Patel Industries Limited, (iv) M/s Sipani Automobiles Limited.

On the basis of discussions with all the parties, the Committee determined that except M/s Sipani Automobiles Limited, others were interested only in buying the machinery. M/s Sipani on the other hand, intended to operate the plant and manufacturing automobile engines. The Committee, therefore, recommended that an agreement to convert ATL into joint sector may be entered into with M/s Sipani Automobiles Limited (SAL). The main provisions of the joint venture agreement approved by the Government were:

(i) M/s ATL will be converted into a joint sector enterprise. The State Government will reduce its shareholding to 26% and transfer 25% of shares to Sipani Automobiles. The balance 49% will be sold to public.

(ii) M/s Sipani will pay Rs. 5.55 crores in consideration for 74% equity. They will retain 25% of the 75-lakh shares and sell 49% shares to dealers and public. Of Rs. 5.55 crores to be paid by the private promoter, Rs. 3.8 crores will be paid within 4-6 months and the balance 1.7 crores within 12 months of the date of the agreement.

(iii) The State Government will reinvest Rs. 4.55 crores as secured loan and pay interest at 12% per annum. The principal will be repaid in 5 annual installments after a moratorium of 3 years.

(iv) M/s ATL will prepare a balance sheet as on 31.3.911 showing the liabilities of the company and the State Government will assume all repayment liabilities of loans/interest except the liabilities on account of working capital upto Rs. 2.30 crores. The State Government will also bear all dues of sales tax, central excise, municipal/panchayat taxes and electricity dues on the date of the agreement.

(v) There will be no further inflow of funds from the St ate Government to ATL in future. The State Government will also not give any guarantee for any funds to be raised in future by ATL.

(vi) M/s Sipani Automobiles Limited will operate ATL for a minimum period of 9 years or till they repay all the dues to the Government.

(vii) SAL and ATL will engage workers at their discretion. SAL agree to re-employ about 600-700 employees within one year of the date of signing of the agreement and increase it to 1000. However, M/s SAL and ATL shall have exclusive right to employ any personnel of their choice for running the unit.

It is apparent that the impulse to bring about a change in ownership and managerial organisation of the two undertakings was because of large losses incurred by them over a number of years. In both the cases there were problems in the choice of technology and location, and failure of the management's to provide credible leadership, interference by the State Government and inability of the enterprises to raise sufficient resources for fresh investment, these enterprises are located in backward district and posting as Chief Executive of these units was not considered as an important position for senior civil servants. The result was that most of the time persons posted to these organisations were trying to get out. Politicians used these enterprises to enhance their influence by distributing jobs and favours. In this way they were seeking to maximize their power and perquisites rather than improving the welfare of the citizens. The interest of the Corporations was far removed from their mind. With indifference leadership provided by the management, many officials of the Corporations are reported to have developed business interests in these enterprises. In this way politician, executives as well as workers' leaders benefited from these enterprises. The loser was the State exchequer, which continued to support these units by meeting their cash requirements. Having decided that it was no longer viable to operate UPSCC and ATL as State enterprises, the State Government did not adopt a uniform approach for divesting ownership of these enterprises. In case of ATL, the Government closed down the unit, gave labour and management terminal benefits and then started looking for options to dispose off the assets. In implementing this decision they were fully supported by the Board of Directors of ATL. In case of UPSCC the plants continued to operate, while the options for transfer of State Government shares were being discussed. Some nominees of the State Government on the Board of Directors of UPSCC were not committed to the idea of privatisation. Many of them are reported to have cast doubt on the appropriateness of this decision. They felt that the operations of the Corporation could be improved and there was no need to divest State ownership. This situation could have been corrected if the Board of Directors of the Corporation was re-constituted with those who were committed to support such a decision. Also the key officials of the Corporation were not closely associated in the discussions for considering different modes or the terms on which State Government shares were transferred. No consultation was held with workers' representative at any state. Their views were not invited either on the reasons for the losses suffered by the Corporation or on the mode of privatization. This gave the impression that the Government was unmindful of the workers' interests. The transfer of management to M/s Dalmias had to be effected with political assistance. This was done just before the assembly elections and the haste with which the operations were concluded and the manner of take over by the private promoters creased the impression that undue favours were being shown to them.

In case of UPSCC agreement was reached with M/s Dalmia hey they would acquire 51% shareholding in UPSCC. However, in view of the Court Order prohibiting sale of assets of UPSCC, 49% shares with book value of Rs. 33.45 crores were transferred to them. At 75% the value of these shares was assessed at Rs. 25.09 crores Dalmia paid Rs. 5 crores in cash. It was agreed that the balance of Rs. 20.09 crores would be paid by them within 24 months. This cash would not accrue to the State exchequer but would be reinvested as loan to UPSCC to be repaid by them over nine years. The loans extended by the State Government and liabilities of the State agencies were limited to Rs. 25 crores. These will be repaid over 8 year's period. The State Government also agreed to write off sales tax liability of Rs. 1.14 crores and stamp duty of Rs. 11 lakhs. On the outstanding loans to the financial institutions amounting to about Rs. 100 crores, no commitment was given by the State Government and the liability of the Corporation would continue.

In case of ATL State Government's contribution was Rs. 7.50 crores. In addition they had extended long term loan of Rs. 5.13 crores and Rs. 27.41 crores to meet cash losses. SAL agreed to pay Rs. 5.55 crores of which Rs. 4.5 crores was to be reinvested by the State Government over a period of 8 years. The State Government transferred ATL for Rs. 1 crore of cash and Rs. 4.55 crores as loan. Unlike in case of UPSCC the State Government agreed to take over all dues of sales tax, excise electricity dues etc.

Another major difference in the two agreements was with regard to the liability towards workers. In case of UPSCC, the Government had insisted that all the workers would have to be employed by the new management, but in ATL M/s Sipani made it clear that while preference would be given to erstwhile ATL employees they would employ only as many workers as was considered necessary by them.

A few lessons emerge from this review. First, there are many obstacles to privatization like developing a coherent strategy, choosing enterprises, valuation of assets, finding credible entrepreneurs capable of successfully running the enterprises. Second, there is need for transparency in the privatization process. This may be overlooked in the interest of speed. But if the consideration of alternative modes of privatization, valuation of assets, and selection of new owners is open, the potential for allegation of irregularities, collusion of corruption would be less. If some special concessions are to be granted to the owners, it is even more important that the process is transparent. Third, the bidding for private loss making enterprises may attract very few private promoters. This may done due to an apprehension that even after divesting ownership the Government would not allow the enterprises to operate freely. These may also be a perception that the Government had decided as to whom they would prefer to sell their shareholding and the exercise of selection was only a formality. In both UPSCC and ATL although a number of business groups showed interest to take over, they dropped out and only one group each was left. Fourth even in advanced countries with sophisticated financial markets it is difficult to determine the market value of the assets of loss making enterprises. After years of decreasing investment and inadequate maintenance it may be almost impossible to reach universally acceptable estimate of value of assets. In developing countries, this task is even more difficult. In order to assess their value, all assets of the unit proposed to be privatised should be catalogued. Once a list of plant and machinery is prepared, it should be valued at realistic market price. Since expertise for this type of work is not likely to be available in the Government, this task may be assigned to professional appraisers. In case of UPSCC no such catalogue of assets was prepared. M/s Billmoria & Co. estimated the value of assets mainly on the basis of Annual Reports and Audited Balance Sheets of the Corporation. This led to complaints that assets were under-valued and undue favours were shown to M/s Dalmias. Fifth, there is a strong inertia to change the system. The opposition to change comes from the managers of such enterprises. They would like to keep the enterprise in the public sector regardless of its performance. Opposition may also come for civil servants that are deputed to work in public enterprises. Sixth, it requires imagination and drive to implement the divestiture of State ownership. In fact, besides the finance departments, there may be very few supporters of privatization in the Government. A lobby, therefore, should be created to support the process. For this it would be necessary to demonstrate to the civil servants and political executive the gains to the economy by the State transferring the ownerships of enterprises. Seventh, in the privatization process workers should invariably be consulted. Workers feel that the decision to divest State ownership is taken primarily to reduce their number. They will be the only losers and would have to bear the burden of rationalization and adjustment. In many cases workers have agreed to bear a part of the adjustment cost. This is so when they feel that the decisions are equitable and they are not being unfairly treated. Eighth, it may be better to close down the unit, give labour their legitimate compensation and then proceed with the transfer of ownership to private groups. Governments are generally unwilling to close down the enterprises they own. However, in cases where surplus workers are in large numbers and their leadership unable to reach a settlement, this may be the only viable option. In case of ATL, Government reached the conclusion that the business of the Corporation could not be carried out profitably. They, therefore, shut down the operations. The transfer of ownership did not create opposition even though in this case the new owners decided to re-employ only half the number of erstwhile employees at ATL, Lastly, the transfer of ownership of large enterprises is not a routine decision. It can be implemented successfully in a stable political environment and when there is no doubt about government's fairness. When elections are about to be held, it would be best to postpone decisions on such issues.

4

Valuation of Shares of State Level Public Enterprises – An Illustrative Case*

The valuation decisions have become critical to successful implementation of privatization programmes. There is a need to introduce a great deal of transparency about them. A good valuation decisions benefits both the buyer and seller. It goes a long-way in creating an environment of mutual trust which is an essential pre-requisite to settle the negotiations for the sale or transfer of an SLPE. This paper proposes to undertake valuation of Hyderabad Allwyn Ltd. To show as to how the best price for transfer or sale could be decided in the case of an SLPE. This paper proposes to undertake valuation of Hyderabad Allwyn Ltd. To show as to how the best price for transfer of sale could be decided in the case of an SLPE.

The success of any privatization exercise would depend on the terms on which the transfer of ownership or effective management was effected. Optimally, this should have given the best possible financial inflow to the government. While ensuing that the enterprise privatized serve the best

---

* R.Nandagopal, R.K.Mishra SLPE Working Group, Institute of Public Enterprise, OU Campus, Hyderabad-500 07.

management for it's continued operation. For serving the best taken in such privatization exercises, the key factor is valuation of assets. The valuation of company's assets is as complex issue and often proves to be the stage that delays the pace of the reforms and privatization in the SLPEs. The case of the Uttar Pradesh Cement Corporation Ltd. has aroused a great deal of interest among the students and practitioner of valuation. The difference on this has become the critical element affecting the transferring of ownership of the SLPE to private sector. The process of valuation resorted to a final value and opted has been criticized as leading to the enterprise being under-sold. As a result, the party in power had to stall the decision.

The case of the Uttar Pradesh Auto Tractors Ltd. has also come into a sharp criticism because of inadequate transparency about the price at which the company was sold to M/s Sipani Automotive Ltd. This case has highlighted the urgency and need to strengthen the valuation skills and negotiating capability of the policy makers and implementers.

This requires, among other things, sound knowledge of various valuation methods and their application.

The paper proposes to illustrate the various methods of valuation with reference to a specific case. HAL is an SLPE in the engineering sector. The State Government has taken decision that HAL should be sold to the private sector. Through the applications various techniques and a range of possible prices at which it could be done, could be compared.

About HAL

HAL was incorporated in January 1942 as a joint venture in a southern state. After two decades of its existence, it was brought into the field of the managing agents and was managed by them for a decade. Subsequently, the company became an SLPE.

Profile of HAL

The company has six product divisions. Its refrigerator

division manufactures domestic refrigerators, deep freezers, air-conditioners and water coolers. It has the technology back from M/s Hitachi, Japan. The company's auto division produces passenger bus body and mini-bus bodies. The appliances division of the company produces the domestic LPG cylinders and steel furniture. The company's watch division produces watchcases and watches. It has technological collaboration from M/s Seiko, Japan. The machinery division of the company produces s all-cut-band saw machines and industrial sewing machines. M/s Mitaubishi Electric Company, Japan is giving the technological support to this division. One of the company's subsidiary, Allwyn Nissan Ltd. producing light commercial vehicles was sold out to a private company Mahindra and Mahindra in 1989. The total income of the company increased from Rs. 42 crores in 1981-82 to Rs. 196 crores in 1989-90. Against a profit of Rs. 3 crores in 1998-90, the company incurred a loss of Rs. 36 crores in 1990-91. Though the company aimed at tighter financial management, increased productivity and wider product appeal and acceptability in 1990-91, the emerging reality turned out to be worse than expected for a variety of reasons. The company is in a deep morass and its chances of turnaround have been rated very low. The State Government has initiated steps to privatize the concern.

Valuation of HAL

In the literature on valuation of firms' reference has been made to the following five distinct methods viz., 1) Net Tanagible Asset Method 2) Stock Exchange Method 3) Earning Capacity Value Method 4) Fair Value Method, and 5) Face Value Plus Interest Method.

Net Tangible Assets Method

The net tangible assets value is computed with the help of the latest audited balance sheet. First, the figure of the assets is worked out. As a second step, the balances in respect of current liabilities, long term debt, intangibles including goodwill and assets to be written-off are then deducted from the total assets. In the third stage, the assets are revalued and any increase or decrease on account of this has to be effected. The ultimate figure arrived at gives the value of the net tangible asset. Dividing net tangible assets arrives at the net tangible asset per share by the number of shares with the company. While computing the net asset value certain points have to be given due credit. The new bonus issue and the fresh issue of equity should be taken into account while computing the net tangible asset per share. Any reserves, which have not been created out of genuine profits, should not be taken into account. The provisions for any other terminal benefits to the employees should be deducted as liabilities. In other words, this method equates the value of the firm to the net-worth of the business. The contingent liabilities, which impair the net worth of the company, will have to be deducted from the assets of the company.

One of the limitations of the net-tangible assets method is that it does not show the true book value of the assets if they have not been revalued in the recent past. Similarly, if a firm does not follow a sound depreciation policy, the net tangible asset method will not provide a fair valuation. The value of net tangible asset per share was Rs. 18.89 in 1989-90 for the HAL as shown below in Table 3.1

Table 4.1 Net Tangible Assets Method

Year	*86-87*	*87-88* *17 months*	*89-90* *15 months*
Book Value per Share (Rs.)	22.37	22.45	18.89

Stock Exchange Method

The stock exchange method can be used only in such cases where the companies are listed on one or more stock exchanges. There have been some cases of both the Central and State enterprises being listed on the stock exchanges. These enterprises earlier belonged to private sector. The stock exchange method is very easy to understand and operate. In this method, the market value acts as the guiding factor for valuation of shares. The underlying principle is that the market presents a genuine assessment of the managerial and economic strengths of the enterprise through pricing of its scrips on day-to-day basis. This method is said to have a high element of objectivity. However, it is argued that the market price of the scrips can always be manipulated, especially with the help of the information that insiders have about the probable course, which is likely to take place in respect of the ownership transfer of a company. This can however be overcome by averaging out the prices of the scrips of a company for a period ranging from three months to three years. This method was widely used while nationalizing private undertakings sin the United Kingdom and India. Another way to overcome this problem is to take high and low values of the shares over a period time and then averaged out them. Table 3.2 shows the valuation of the company as per the stock exchange method. The table shows that the average market value per share of the company was Rs. 15.92 in 1990.

Table 4.2 Market Value Method

Year	*High Rs.*	*Low Rs.*	*Average Rs.*
1988	21.00	7.50	14.25
1989	22.00	12.00	17.00
1990	18.02*	13.83*	15.92

* High and Low values of the year 1990 calculated by taking Averages of High and Low market values of 12 months.

$$\text{Share Value} = \frac{14.25 + 1. + 15.92}{3} = \text{Rs. } 15.72$$

Profit Earning Capacity Value Method

Profit earning capacity value method suggests the

valuation of the company by capitalizing the average of profits after tax. According to the guidelines issued by the Controller of Capital Issues of India, the capital Issues of India, the capitalisation of profits for in various lines of operation could be done on the following basis:

- 15 per cent on capital employed in the case of manufacturing concerns.
- 20 per cent in the case of trading companies and a trading company is a such company which derives from trading activity a turnover of more than 40 but not exceeding 60 per cent
- 17.5 per cent in the case of intermediate companies

In the case of manufacturing enterprises exceptions may have to be made to the capitalization rate of 15 per cent. If there is a staggering difference between the market price and the price arrived at 15 per cent of capitalisation rate. It would be advisable to have a higher rate of capitalisation for negotiating prices at which the enterprise can be transferred to the private sector. In the case of well diversified and multi-product enterprises, it is advisable to change something over and above 15 per cent of capitalisation rate. It must be ensured that the profits shown in audited accounts of the company are true profits completely showed of window-dressing. Normally, a period of 3 years is taken to average out the profits. If the profits of the last three years are stable, they may be averaged out on the basis of the simple arithmetic mean. However, if the profits are rising year after year steadily, it is useful to take the help of weighted average method. It is very easy to apply this method. However, the only difficulty with the profit earning capacity value method is selecting an appropriate capitalisation rate. Table 3 shows the profit earning capacity value at 15 per cent capitalisation rate for HAL. It was Rs. 13.97 per share for 1989-90 as per the simple arithmetic mean. It was Rs. 14.63 during the same period as per the waited average mean. It was Rs. 10.53 under simple arithmetic mean for five years at 15 per cent capitalisation rate.

Table 4.3 Earning capacity Value (under simple average method) at capitalisation rate

	86-87	*87-88 17 months*	*89-90 15 months*
Net Profit (in Lakhs)	347	448	362
No. of Shares	81,03,837	81,03,837	1,84,00,206

Average of 3 years net profit =

$$\frac{347+448+362}{3} = \text{Rs. } 385.666666 \text{ Lakhs}$$

Share value of 15% of capitalisation rate =

$$\frac{38566666 \times 100}{1{,}84{,}00{,}206 \times 15} = \text{Rs. } 13.97$$

Table 4.4 Earning Capacity Value (under weighted average method) at 15 % of Capitalisation Rate

	86-87	*87-88 17 months*	*89-90 15 months*
1. Net Profit (in Lakhs)	347	448	362
2. Weights (product of 1 and 2)	1	2	3
No. of Shares	81,03,837	81,03,837	1,84,00,206

Weighted Average of 3 years Net Profit =

$$\frac{347+896+1086}{6} = \frac{2329}{6} = 388.1666 \text{ Lakhs}$$

The share value of 15 % Capitalisation Rate:

$$\frac{388.1666 \times 100}{1{,}84{,}.00{,}206 \times 15} = \text{Rs. } 14.63$$

Table 4.5 Share value under Simple Average Method for 5 years Net Profits at 15% of Capitalisation rate

	1984-85	*1985-86*	*1986-87*	*1987-88 17 months*	*1988-89 15 months*
1. Net Profit (in Lakhs)	275	296	347	448	362

Average of 5 years Net Profit s : 345.6 Lakhs

Share value of 15% Capitalisation Rate :

$$\frac{3456000 \text{ X}100}{1,84,00,2063 \text{ X } 15} = \text{Rs. } 12.52$$

Fair Value Method

The fair value method is determined on the basis of the average net tangible asset value and the profit earned capacity value. The Controller of Capital Issue of India has noted this method for valuation of shares. The fair value according to the guidelines issued by the Controller of Capital Issues is computed by re-working the profit earned capacity value. However, in the case of companies, having the average of net tangible assets value and profit earning capacity value capitalized at 15 per cent rate turning out to be not below 20 per cent of the average market price, there is no need to rework the profits. In case the average of the net tangible asset per share value and profit earning capacity per share value is less than the average market price by over 20 per cent, the profit earning capacity value is reworked by modified capitalisation rate upto a maximum of 8 per cent. According to the Controller of Capital Issue if the profit earning capacity value is nil, the fair value should be limited to half of the net asset value. If, however, the net assets constitute mostly liquid assets, the fair value may be fixed upto 63 per cent of the tangible asset value. The fair value method gives a more balanced method of valuation of the production potential and income generating abilities of the assets of a company.

Table 4 shows the fair value of the shares of HAL for the year 1989-90 as Rs. 16.48, which struck a golden mean between the net tangible assets of value per share of Rs. 18.89 and the profit earning capacity value per share of Rs. 13.97 during the same period.

Table 4.6 Fair Value method

a. Net assets value per share during the year 1989-90 = Rs. 18.90

b. Earning capacity value (under weighted average method) of 15% capitalisation rate = Rs. 14.06

$$\text{Fair value} = \frac{a+b}{2} = \frac{18.90+14.06}{2} = \text{Rs. } 16.48$$

Face Value Plus Interest Method

According to this method the valuation of the firm is done by taking into consideration its total investment at the time of acquisition and by adding to the same an equivalent of 15 per cent rate interest every year. From the total sum so computed, total amount of dividends paid to shareholders form the date of acquisition stretching to the date of valuation has to be deducted. The remainder is divided by total number of shares to compute the value per share of the company. This method is suitable for the valuation of companies, which have a non-volatible, assured income stream. The method turns out to be very useful even for such companies which make capital additions now and then only. It is not useful in the case of enterprises having a negative net worth. Table 5 shows that the share value of HAL as per this principle was Rs. 53.70 in 1989-90.

Table 4.6 Face Value plus Interest Method

The year of acquisition of company by the Govt. = May 1975.

The total paid-up capital during 1974-75 = 180,49,170

The total number of shares during 1974-75 = 1804917 of Rs. 10 each

Compound Interest on Total paid-up capital 15% from 1975 June

Compound Interest formula: $A=P(1+R)^n$

Where A= Amount, P= Principal, R = rate of Interest, n =number of years

A= P+I= Principal +Interest

Compound Interest on total paid up capital from May 1975 to 1990

$A= 1,80,49,170(1+10.15)^{29/2}$

take logs : $\log A = \log 1,80,49,170 + \frac{29 \log 1.15}{2}$

$$\log A = 7.25640 + \frac{29}{2} \times 0.06070$$

$\log A = 7.25640 + 0.88015$

$\log A = 8.13650$

A = anti-log of 8013650

A = 13,69,30,000

Approximately total dividend paid from 1974-75 to 1989-90 = 400 lakhs

Share value =

$$\frac{13,69,30,000-4,00,00,000}{18,04,917} = \frac{9,69,30,000}{18,04,917} = \text{Rs. } 53.70$$

Share value of Hyderabad Allwyn Ltd. as per Face Value plus Interest Method = Rs. 53.70

Discussion

The application of the various methods of valuation points out that the value per share in the case of HAL fluctuated between a low of Rs. 14 as computed on the basis of profit earning capacity value method to a high of Rs. 18.89 as computed on the basis of net- tangible assets method. The valuation done on the basis of face value plus interest method (interest at 15 per cent per annum) was Rs. 53.70 be made, Why is there a big difference between the value per share as evidenced by this method and those indicated by the other methods? If the assets of HAL are revalued, there is every likelihood that the so-called difference will not be there at all. For the revaluation of assets assistance of valuers will have to be taken. The value given by the stock-exchange method cannot be taken as the basis to negotiate the transfer of the undertaking from the public to private sector as the trading of shares of the company is very limited since the state government holds more than 66 per cent of the share capital.

To sum up, the study about the valuation of HAL brings out the following lessons:

1. The SLPE s should have sound accounting systems
2. The accounts should be recast to adjust the impact of undesired accounting policies.
3. An information base should be created to collect relevant information about similar enterprise operating in the private sector
4. The valuation should be done on the basis of various methods. A balanced approach should be followed in striking the transfer price to private sector. The approach should be crystal-clear and fully objective.

5

Public Sector Reforms in Rajasthan – Reforms and Privatisation*

At the time when the State of Rajasthan ushered into planning era, infrastructural base, both social as well as economic, was virtually non-existent. This necessitated Government's intervention, through agency of public sector, in critical areas of the State's economy, and consequently led phenomenal growth of State Level public enterprises (SLPEs) both in number and size. The number of public enterprises which was only 8 at the end of 1960 increased over last 10 years by more than 200% (Rs. 912 crores in 1980-81 to Rs. 2969 crores at the end of 1980-90)

Before State public enterprises came on the horizon, role of the state was confined primarily to public utilities such as electricity, transportation pursued as departmental activities. Today dominant existence to public sector is evident in almost all-critical areas of the State's economy. About half of the enterprises are engaged in manufacturing activity like sugar, mining, electronics, textiles, and chemicals. The remaining enterprises are engaged in the activities relating to electricity, tourism, and warehousing, agricultural inputs, dairy, housing,

* Ashok Haldia, Joint Advisor (Financial), Government of Rajasthan, Bureau of Public Enterprises.

transportation, tribal area development, scheduled caste development. Some of the act as financial institutions. While these enterprises function on commercial basis, their existence was necessitated primarily for playing promotional and developmental role meeting social economic objectives of the Government policies. Diversified nature of State public enterprises has helped not only in building up a sound infrastructural base but also contributed significantly in harnessing growth potential in the related areas.

The sectoral composition of State public enterprise under:

Manufacturing	18
Financial	3
Trading & Service	6
Promotional	8
Welfare	4
Electricity	1
Passenger Transportation	1
	41

The above classification is broad and indicative as many of the enterprises pursue activities, which could be covered under more than one group.

It may be added that Central public sectors undertakings the States are hardly any. The number of such undertaking in the State at the end of 1989-90 was only 6 with total investment (gross block) of Rs.1717 crores. On the basis of investment in Central public sector undertaking in different States, Rajasthan ranked 13th.

The list of State public enterprises in Rajasthan appears at Annexure 'A'. It includes 7 Statutory Corporations /Boards, 16 companies registered under Companies Act, 14 co-operative Societies registered under Cooperative Societies Act 1965. 4 undertaking run departmentally. Of the 16 Companies, 8 wholly owned by the State Government.

A major portion (86.2%) of the total investment in State Public enterprises accounted for 5 enterprises. These are Rajasthan State Electricity Board (Rs. 1861.03 crores), Rajasthan Financial Corporation (Rs. 352.58 crores), Rajasthan Industrial Development & Investment Corporation Ltd. (Rs. 160.36 crores), Rajasthan Housing Board (Rs. 100.32 crores), Rajasthan State Electricity Board alone accounted for 59.67% of additional investment (Rs. 2057 crores) in public enterprises over the last 10 years. The pattern of investment suggests that the aggregate performance of State public enterprises in Rajasthan be mainly depended on productive utilisation of resources in above 5 enterprises.

The State Government has been the main contributor to the total investment made in public enterprises. Its share which was 56.8% at the end of 1980-81 has, however, one down to 42.36% of the additional resources raised by enterprises during 1989-90 period.

Additional investment amounting to Rs. 940 crores in the three years was deployed for financing additions (net) to fixed assets (Rs. 647 crores). The balance of Rs. 293 crores has wiped off by accumulated losses or is represented by intangibles.

The trend in performance of public enterprises in Rajasthan is not much different from general state of public sector performance elsewhere. State enterprises in aggregate terms have been incurring losses year after year. Amount of loss incurred has, however, fluctuated from year to year. The loss incurring in 1986-87, 1987-88, 1988-89 and 1989-90 was Rs. 20.60, 99.56, 64.12 and 150.56 crores respectively.

The over all financial performance of State enterprises is mainly dependent on the level of performance of Rajasthan State Electricity Board which incurred loss of Rs. 8.99 crores in 1986-87, Rs. 168.61 crores in 1989-90at the end of each of the above years respectively, at the end of 1989-90, RSEB of alone accounted for 78.53% accumulated loss incurred by the State enterprises. If figures of financial performance of RSEB are excluded the remaining enterprises have shown improvement in their performance in as much as that these have earned profit for the first time of Rs. 10.27 crores during 1988-89 and subsequently of Rs. 17.60 crores in 1989-90.

Enterprise wise figures of financial performance (profit / loss excluding prior year adjustment) is indicated at Annexure 'B'. It would be observed that 13 enterprises incurred losses continuously for last 3 years. Prominent among these ate Rajasthan State Electricity Board, Rajasthan State Agro Industries Corporation, Rajasthan State Tungsten Development Corporation, Rajasthan Electronics Ltd. and Rajasthan Small Industries Corporation. On the other hand, the enterprises such as Rajasthan Financial Corporation, Rajasthan Housing Board, Rajasthan State Mines and Minerals Ltd., Rajasthan State Mineral Development Corporation, Rajasthan State Hotels Corporation, Rajasthan State Bridges and Construction Corporation, Rajasthan State Water Resources Development Corporation and Rajasthan Rajya Bunkar Sahkari Sangh earned profit regularly in the last three years. 16 enterprises had accumulated losses aggregating to Rs. 708.03 crores at the end of 1989-90. Bulk of this was accounted for by Rajasthan State Electricity Board (RS 556.03 crores), Rajasthan State Road Transport Corporation (Rs. 37.32 crores), Rajasthan Land Development Corporation (Rs. 15.72 crores), Rajasthan Cooperative Dairy Federation (Rs. 38.14 crores) and Rajasthan State Agro Industries Corporation (Rs. 8.91 crores).

It may be appropriate to add that the contribution made by the State Public Enterprise to the Government has increased progressively from Rs. 101.12 crores in 1985-86 to Rs. 185.27 crores in 1989-90. Item wise break-up of such contribution made 1989-90 is given below:

	Amount in Rs. Crores
Royalty	3.75
Income Tax	4.30
Sales Tax	2.44
Excise Duty	41.80

(Contd...)

Cess	0.15
Dividend	0.94
Interest on Govt. capital and Interest on loans in case of RSEB	88.55
Others	43.34
	185.27

While there is no denial to fact that State Public Enterprise has made significant contribution in accelerating the pace of economic development of the State and their financial performance (excluding RSEB) in aggregate terms have shown improvement in the recent years, the fact remains that many of these enterprises are incurring losses year after year. 14 enterprises are incurred losses during 1989-90. Net worth of about 14 enterprises has either become negative or eroded by more than 50%. An insight into enterprise wise performance reveals that some of these have not been able to purse their corporate existence as a State level institution. Unsatisfactory performance can be attributed to infrastructural bottle necks, lower capacity utilisation and productivity level, poor financial management, unremunerative tariff / prices, absence of proper work culture etc.

The State of performance has underlined the need for change in approach as well as practices adopted for the growth of public sector and its management. Needless to add that the limited financial resources of the Government can hardly land further support to loss making units at the cost of other pressing economic priorities. In order to make State Public sector healthy and vibrant it size need to be rationalized and management of public enterprise infused with dynamism and made more accountable for utilisation of productive resources at their disposal. At the same time, the fact that public sector enterprises are functioning under whole lot of constraints needs to be appreciated and concerted efforts made for resolving this so as to enable enterprises functioning on professional / commercial lines.

The State Government concerned with the State performance of State public enterprises has initiated thorough analysis and critical review of growth, structure and organizational pattern of State public enterprises and of policy and practices adopted, at the enterprise level as well as Governmental level, in managing these enterprises. Realising that haphazard growth of public sector irrespective of the need and desirability of Government's intervention and participation has to be curbed no new enterprise has been set up in the recent years. Rajasthan State Cooperative Oil Seeds Growers Federation (Tilam Sangh) has been formed with effect from 1.4.90 as measure reorganization, by taking over oil seed processing units of Rajasthan State Cooperative Marketing Federation.

A Fresh look is being given at the Governmental Level on continued existence of some of the State public enterprises their units / activities considering state of financial performance in the past and need for continued governmental intervention and participation in a dynamic context. Accordingly, on that basis Government has already taken decisions with regard to alternative options available in respect of some of the enterprises. About one fourth of the total enterprises have been subjected to major surgical measures. Rajasthan State Tanneries ltd. has been decided to be wound up. Proposals are under consideration for sale by transfer of Government equity in private sector. Rajasthan Rajya Van Vikas Nigam Ltd. has been closed down. Incase of Rajasthan State Agro Industries corporation, the Cabinet has recently authorized the Chief Minister for taking a decision for its closure or otherwise. Wollen Yarn manufacturing units of Rajasthan Small Industries Corporation have been closed down and action for their disposal is being taken. Bikaner Wollen Mills a closed public enterprise has been put to sale by tender.

An agreement has been enter into with Instrumentation Ltd. Kota for transfer of Rajasthan Electronics Ltd. The tungsten activity of Rajasthan State Tungsten Development Corporation along with its assets, liabilities and manpower has been transferred to Hindustan Zinc Ltd. Sulphide factory of Rajasthan State Chemical works, Didwana has been given on lease basis to entrepreneur in private sector. Similarly, a Sodium Sulphate plant of another departmental unit has been decided to be given of lease basis. In case of Rajasthan Government Salt Works (Pachpadra) Government is considering the proposal for restricting its role to development of salt area and allowing pan holders to take up production and marketing of salt at their own. In case of Rajasthan Land Development corporation, which has outlined its utility, while corporate entity has been decided to be continued, organizational new worth and manpower is being reduced to minimum.

In addition, BPE has examined the need and feasibility of rehabilitation of 5 more enterprises, which are incurring losses or whose existence has not served the State in any significant manner.

At the enterprise level initiatives have been taken in closing down loss making activities/units or giving them in the private sector on lease/contract basis. Some of the initiatives taken are catering services, to the private sector in some of the units of Rajasthan Tourism Development Corporation Ltd. and Rajasthan State hotels Corporation Ltd. Closure of uneconomic mines by Rajasthan State Mineral Development Corporation; entrusting mining operation to private sector contractors; entrusting cold storage/ice plant on lease basis by Rajasthan State Co-operative Marketing Federation; increasing proportion of hired buses and rationalization of plying of buses on different routes by Rajasthan State Road Transport Corporation.

State Government has recently constituted a Committee comprising of non-officials representing different political parties and officials for making suggestions for improvement in performance of State public enterprises and for closure of loss making enterprises, the committee has already considered the possibility for alternative options in respect of 4 State public enterprises.

In case of enterprises which are to function in the public

sector, Government is making concerted efforts for bringing about improvement in their performance a part from the Committee constituted, as stated above, a study on growth and management of State public enterprises in Rajasthan has been entrusted to National Council of Applied Economic Research. Scope of the study includes all aspects concerning public sector functioning. The Government has reconstituted in October 1984 Bureau of Public enterprises under the Chairmanship of Chief Secretary to oversee functioning of State public enterprises with a view to bring about improvement in their performance. Towards this end BPE has undertaken detailed review of working of 35 enterprises (including second evaluation of 15 enterprises). Accordingly, specific suggestions have been made for bringing about improvement in various functional areas. These cover not only improvement in capital structure and working capital management but also increase in capacity utilisation, cost reduction, productivity improvement, modernization technological up-gradation and innovation. BPE has also laid emphasis on systems improvement. Some of the initialization taken are:

- Preparation of Corporate plan by State public enterprises.
- Preparation of action plan by loss making enterprises with a view to bring about turn around improvement in performance.
- Financial restructuring in case of enterprise whose capital structure has become highly im-balanced. Emphasis on obtaining funds to the extent possible from financial institutions/banks/other resources instead of relying on budgetary support from the State Government.
- Up dating technology and production methods in enterprises operating with outdated and/or sub-optimal technology.
- Emphasis on proper manpower planning. BPE has evolved a mechanism for absorption of surplus

employees of more public enterprises in other public enterprises Voluntary Retirement Scheme has also evolved.

As in the case of Central public sector undertaking State level public enterprises in Rajasthan are at cross road. Their performance in aggregate and individual terms needs improvement. The State government concerned with the nature, size, growth and state of health of these enterprises has taken initiatives involving alternative options such as closure/sale/lease etc. in respect of the enterprises which incurring losses and do not have major socio-economic objective to achieve, and for bringing about turn around improvement performance, both in physical and financial terms, of remaining.

Annexure – A

LIST OF PUBLIC ENTERPRISES UNDER THE PURVIEW OF RAJASTHAN BPE

A – Statutory Corporation / Boards

1. Rajasthan State Electricity Board.
2. Rajasthan State Road Transport Corporation
3. Rajasthan Financial Corporation
4. Rajasthan State Warehousing Corporation
5. Rajasthan Housing Board
6. Rajasthan Land Development Corporation
7. Rajasthan State Agricultural Marketing Board.

B – Registered Companies

8. The Ganganagar Sugar Mills Ltd.
9. Rajasthan State Tanneries Ltd.
10. Rajasthan Mines and Minerals Ltd.
11. Rajasthan State Ind. Devp. And Invest. Corp.

12. Rajasthan State Mineral Development Corp. Ltd.
13. The Rajasthan Small Industries Corp. Ltd.
14. Rajasthan State Hotels Corporation Ltd.
15. Rajasthan Tourism Development Corporation
16. Rajasthan State Seeds Corporation Ltd.
17. Rajasthan State Agro Industries Corporation Ltd.
18. Rajasthan State Bridges and Construction Corporation
19. Rajasthan State Handloom Development Corporation
20. Rajasthan Water Resources Development Corporation
21. Rajasthan Van Vikas Nigam Ltd.
22. Rajasthan Electronics Ltd.
23. Rajasthan State Tungsten Devp. Corp.

C- Registered Co-operative Societies.

24. Rajasthan Coop. Dairy Federation Ltd.
25. Rajasthan Scheduled Caste Coop. Devp. Corp. Ltd.
26. Rajasthan Tribal Area Devp. Coop. Fed. Ltd.
27. Rajasthan State Bunker Shakari Sangh Ltd.
28. Rajasthan State Coop. Sheep & Wool Marketing Fed.
29. Rajasthan Rajya Sahakari Upbhokta Sangh Ltd.
30. Rajasthan State Coop. Marketing Federation Ltd.
31. Rajasthan State Coop. Housing Federation Ltd.
32. Shri Keshorai Patan Sahkari Sugar Mills Ltd.
33. Rajasthan Coop Spinning Mills Ltd.
34. Rajasthan State Cooperative Oil Seed Growers Fed. Ltd.
35. Rajasthan State Cooperative Spinning Mills Ltd., Gulabpura
36. Gangapur Coop. Spinning Mills Ltd.

37. Ganganager Coop Spinning Mills Ltd.
38. Sri Ganganagar Coop Oil seed Processing Ltd.

D- Departmental Undertakings.

39. Rajasthan State Chemical Works Didwana
40. Rajasthan State Chemical Works Didwana
41. Rajasthan Govt. Salt Works Didwana
42. Rajasthan Govt. Salt Works Pachpadra.

6

State Level Public Sector Enterprises in Maharashtra

The PSEs in Maharashtra State consist of entities incorporated under a variety of statutes, e.g., the Companies Act and special Acts of the Central / State Government. The heterogeneity of these enterprises lies also in their objectives and roles. In addition, they differ widely in financial strength, profitability, staffing pattern, area of operation, etc. Further the aggregate position is to a large extent influenced by the performance of a few very large enterprises, such as the Maharashtra State Electricity Board. An undifferentiated comparison of these enterprises may not this be very meaningful. The PSEs have, therefore, been classified into five board groups, viz. Commercial, Commercial- cum- Promotional, Promotional, Financial and Public Utilities. This classification has been shown in Annexure I. (The 41 PSEs listed do not include subsidiaries of such enterprises).

Competition includes greater efficiency. Several PSEs however, operate in non-competitive fields. Many PSEs do not have clearly defined objectives or, in fact, have mutually

A.M.Khan, State Bureau of Public Sector Enterprises, Government of Maharashtra, Finance Department, Mantralaya, Bombay-400 032 inconsistent objectives. Moreover, the capability of these enterprises to function efficiently is often undermined by a host of factors such as lack of autonomy, motivation, etc.. In such an environment, the managers of these PSEs can often not be accountable for results. The way the managers ate selected, trained and rewarded may also not be appropriate for running PSE efficiency. Further, non-viable PSEs are seldom liquidated. In fact, the Government has often taken over, in the public sector, the responsibility of running activities un-viable in the private sector.

The special circumstances in which the PSEs function not, however, be an excuse for indifferent performance. With in the environment in which these PSEs function, it may still be possible to set clear, consistent and attainable objectives. Institutional linkage between these enterprises and the Government can be established in such a way that the interference in the working of these enterprises is avoided and at the same time, Government can be established in such a way that undue interference in the working of these enterprises avoided and at the same time, Government exercises effective control to ensure performance and accountability in keeping the goals set by it for these enterprises.

The State Bureau of Public Enterprises set up in October 1986 is providing guidance in this direction. In this, the role of the Bureau's Advisory Board, constituted in May 1987 under the Chairmanship of Shri. V.G.Rajadhyaksha, former member (Industries and Infrastructure), Planning Commission, has been significant. The Board has so far submitted its Reports to the Government in respect of 10 enterprises.

The general guidelines recommended by the Advisory Board in respect of the objectives, roles and functioning of the PSEs have been accepted by Government and incorporated in Government Resolution, Finance Department, dated 9th December 1989 (reproduced at Annexure – II). On the Advisory Board's recommendation the State Government has decided to appoint professionals and/or persons with experience in the relevant fields to the Boards of State PSEs as part-time Chairman and Member of the Board of Directors, and has standardized the scale of allowances and other facilities due to them. The State Government has also decided in principle, to establish a pool from which the selection of Chief Executives of the PSEs will be made.

With the setting up of the State Bureau of PSEs and the Advisory Board to guide the Bureau, an institutional mechanism now exists for systematically evaluating the PSEs, recommending actions which can lead to improved performance, and monitoring periodically the progress made by the enterprises. The capital budgets of the PSEs are scrutinized in the Bureau, and are to be approved by a committee chaired by the Minister (Finance). During this scrutiny, an attèmpt is made to analyze the performance of each enterprise and suggest remedial action. Through the institutional framework comprising the Administrative Department concerned, the Bureau and the Advisory Board it is proposed to continue periodical reviews of the performance of the enterprises, a part from helping them in the preparation of long term annual plans. It is hoped that these arrangements would not only lead to speedier decision making, but also focus attention on major issues requiring action on the part of the PSEs and the Government.

A sound accounting system requires timely compilation and finalization of accounts : otherwise, it is not possible to the source of adverse financial results, thus preventing timely corrective action. The Companies Act requires companies to finalize their accounts within 180 days of the close of the accounting year. However, accounts of only 14 out of 41 enterprises were upto date as at the end of 1989-90. The position has been improving in Government Companies which are several years in arrears have been seeking, and some have obtained, appointment of Statutory Auditors for more than one year at a time so as to obviate the procedural delays involved in such appointments.

Table 6.1 Composition of Financial Resources Employed by PSEs

	1987-88	1988-89	Addition (Reduction)	1989-90	Addition (Reduction)
a. Total Resources	5,635	6,757	1,122	7,933	1,176
b. Share Capital	460	501	41	616	115
c. Loans	2,595	2,981	386	3,270	289
d. Outside Borrowings :					
1. Long Term	2,493	3,223	730	3,997	774
2. Short Term	87	52	(35)	50	(2)

The increase in the equity and loan contribution of the State Government to the PSEs was about Rs. 404 crore during 1989-90, as against Rs. 427 crore in 1988-89. The enterprises borrowed an additional Rs. 772 crore and Rs. 695 crore during 1989-90 and 1988-89 respectively, most of which were guaranteed by the State Government.

Despite the increased use of financial resources, the combined losses of the PSEs increased sharply from Rs. 11.71 crore in 1988-89 to Rs. 74.74 crore in 1989-90, i.e. by Rs. 63.03 crore (Annexure III). The major factor responsible for the increase in aggregate losses has been the decline in profits of the Maharashtra State Electricity Board by Rs. 25.03 crore and the increase in losses incurred by the Maharashtra State Road Transport Corporation (both public utilities) to the extent of Rs. 43.71 crore. This reflects, among other things, the impact of wage revisions effected in these two organizations, which employ a very large complement of staff. Upward revisions in tariffs and other corrective measures that have since been taken are likely to improve this position, the profitability of the remaining two public utilities has also declined. It may be pointed out, however, that with the exception of commercial-cum- promotional enterprises, whose level of losses has remained more or less constant at around Rs.2.40 crore, the combined performance of other categories of enterprises has improved significantly. The profits of commercial enterprises as a group have increased form Rs. 0.05 crore in 1988-89 to Rs. 2.70 crore in 1989-90, owing mainly to an increase in the profits of the Maharashtra State Warehousing Corporation, CIDCO and the Haffkins Bio-Pharmaceutical Corporation and substantially reduced losses incurred by the Maharashtra State Textile Corporation. The increase in aggregate profits of the financial enterprises has been of the order of Rs. 3.39 crore, with both SICOM and Maharashtra State Financial Corporation posting substantially improved results. The aggregate losses of the promotional enterprises fell from Rs. 711.80 lakh in 1988-89 to Rs. 309.13 lakh in 1989-90, largely due to a substantial reduction in the losses incurred by the Tribal Development Corporation, and some improvement in the performance of the regional Development Corporations as a whole. Thus, excluding the public utilities the remaining PSEs made a combined profit of Rs. 2.19 crores in 1989-90 as against a loss of Rs. 7.85 crore in the previous year, improvement of the order of Rs.10.04 crore resulting from improved performance on the part of 21 out of 37 enterprises.

The total of explicit subsidies extended by the PSEs in 1989-90 amounted to Rs. 51 crore and hidden subsidies to Rs. 895 crore, making a total of Rs. 946 crore. The corresponding figures for 1988-89 were Rs. 24 crore and Rs. 701 crore i.e. a total of Rs.725 crore. The increase in the subsidies has been of the order of Rs. 221 crore, almost entirely on account of hidden subsidies. The bulk of the increase has been on account of an increase the hidden subsidies given by MSEB, which increased by Rs. 164 crore, i.e. from Rs. 678 crore to Rs. 842 crore. However, this has been largely on account of the State Government's policy of charging concessional tariff to agricultural consumers and is partly made good by the State Government.

In its Report, the Ninth Finance Commission has reiterated the need for generation of resources by the PSEs of the States and stipulated a minimum dividend of 5% for the commercial enterprises and 3% for the financial enterprises. As against this, the actual return form these two categories of PSEs during the year 1989-90 was about 0.51 %, as against 0.11% in 1988-89. However, in the case of commercial and financial enterprises, the rate of return on capital employed improved from 4.21% and 0.28% respectively in 1988-89 to 5.17% and 0.74% respectively in 1989-90. The rate of return on shareholders equity also increased form 0.05% and 2.22% respectively in 1988-89 to 2.59% and 5.40% respectively in 1989-90 (Annexure III). Although the actual dividend paid fell far short of the desired level, the significant improvement in the rates of return on capital employed and on shareholders equity obviated, to that extent, the need for additional infusion from the State's resources to support the same level of expansion in capital investment.

On the whole, however, the need for improving the performance of the PSEs continues to remain urgent. The only enterprises, which have no profit element, are the purely promotional ones. All others, including commercial-cum-promotional should show a positive return, using the profits on commercial activities, to the extent necessary, to subsidies the promotional activities. The purely promotional enterprises account for an aggregate loss of only Rs. 3.09 crore, as against the aggregate position is largely owing to the losses incurred by MSRTC, 19 enterprises other than those of a purely promotional character also incurred losses in 1989-90 even in some of the promotional PSEs greater efficiency would laid to a further reduction in their losses. For all the other PSEs, especially commercial and financial enterprises and the public utilities the specified norms of return should become the goal.

Some of the enterprises continue to be unable to meet even administrative expenses from their own incomes. Some of the enterprises have taken recourse to diversion of share capital to meet their administrative cost and/or cash losses. In the cases, this has led inevitably to a distortion in the financial structure of the enterprise. It has, therefore, been decided that the funds to be released by the State Government to the PSEs will clearly segregate the funds extended for the creation of revenue generating assets or meeting margin money requirement from those required for meeting administrative expenditure or reimbursement of cash losses.

There are some loss-making PSEs, which serve a limited, or no public purpose. A study of some of these PSEs has been undertaken by the Bureau with the assistant of the Advisory Board several of them are considered irredeemably non-viable. If they are allowed to continue operations, they will lace an increasingly heavy burden on the State's resources. Government is seriously considering alternatives for dealing with such PSEs. One such alternative is closure/winding up. The State Government has taken a decision to wind up two enterprises (Maharashtra Oil seeds Commercial and Industrial Corporation and Overseas Employment and Export Promotion Corporation of Maharashtra) in 1990. The vital question of providing relief to the employees of PSEs that are to be closed is presently under consideration of the Advisory Board. In the case of a few subsidiary companies, privatisation by way of transfer of assets is being examined. Another alternative will be available once that amendment to the Sick Industrial Companies (Special Provisions) Act bringing Government Companies under its purview is given formal effect.

The 41 State PSEs taken together provide employment to 2,98,957 persons. Of these, 22,744 were in the cadre of officers/ supervisors, while the other cadres totaled 2,76,213. 78% of the total number of persons employed in the commercial enterprises and the remaining 3% in the commercial - cum - promotional, promotional and financial enterprises.

Annexure – I

Table 6.2 Classification of Public Enterprises along with Net Profit / Loss position (1989-90)

Rs. in Lakhs.

Name of the Department	*Commercial*	*Commercial–cum–promotional*	*Promotional*	*Financial*	*Public Utilities*
1	2	3	4	5	6
A. Industries, Energy and Labour Department	1.Maharashtra Electronics Corp. Ltd. (Rs. 138.00)	1. Development Corp. of Konkan Ltd. (Rs. 6.53)	1. Maharashtra Industrial Development Corp. (Rs. 28.28)	1.Maharashtra State Financial Corp (Rs. 187.24)	1.Maharashtra State Electricity Board (Rs. 1447.09)
	2. Maharashtra State Mining Corp. (- Rs. 7.91)	2. Development Corp. of Vidarbha Ltd. (- Rs. 31.87)		2. State Industrial & Investment Corp. Ltd. (+ Rs. 310.07)	
	3. Maharashtra Small Scale Industries Development Corp. Ltd. (Rs. 28.00)	3. Maharashtra Development Corp. (-Rs.14.23)			

(Contd...)

1	2	3	4	5	6
	4. Maharashtra Petrochemicals Corp. Ltd. (Rs. 5.29)	4. Western Maharashtra Development Corp. Ltd. (Rs. 25.30)			
		5. Leather Industries Develop. Corp. of Maharashtra (- Rs. 13.66)			
Total of Departments	4(+ Rs. 163.38)	5(+ Rs. 27.93)	1(Rs. 28.28)	2(Rs.497.31)	1(Rs. 1447.09)
B. Agriculture, Animal Husbandry, Dairy Development and Fisheries Dep.	5. MAFCO Ltd. (- Rs. 58.08)				
	6. Maharashtra Agro Industries Development Corp. Ltd. (+Rs. 88.82)	6. Maharashtra Medhi Va Shela Vikas Mahamandal Ltd. (-Rs. 6.71)			

(Contd...)

1	2	3	4	5	6
	7. Maharashtra State Seeds Corp. (- Rs. 33.11)	7.Maharashtra Fisheries Development Corp. Ltd. (- Rs. 10.48)			
Total of the Departments	3(-Rs. 2.99)	2(-Rs. 11.19)			
C. Urban Development Departments	8. City & Industrial Development Corp. of Maharashtra Ltd. (Rs. 51.09)				2.Maharashtra Water Supply and Sewerage Board (Rs. 214.97)
Total of the Departments	1(Rs. 51.09)				1(214.97)
D. Co-operation and Textile Development	9. Maharashtra state Textile Corp. Ltd. -Rs.161.02	8. Maharashtra State Handloom Corp. Ltd. - Rs.126.91			
	10. Maharashtra State Warehousing	9. Maharashtra State Powerloom Corp. Ltd.			

(Contd...)

1	2	3	4	5	6
	Corp. Ltd. Rs. 322.76	-Rs. 32.56			
	11. Maharashtra State Oilseeds Commercial and Industrial Corp. Ltd. -Rs. 350.73				
Total of the Departments	3(-Rs. 188.99)	2(-Rs. 199.49)			
E. Tribal Development			2 Maharashtra State Co-operative Tribal Dev. Corp. Ltd.		
Total for the Department			1(-Rs. 52.20)		
F. Social Welfare, cultural affairs, sports and Tourism Development	12. Maharashtra film stage and cultural devel. Corp. Ltd. -Rs. 17.6	10. Kolhapur Chitraghari Mahamandal Ltd. -Rs. 8.35	3. Lokshahir Annabahui sathe Dev. Corp. Ltd. -Rs. 10.25		

(Contd...)

1	2	3	4	5	6
		11. Maharashtra Tourism Devlo. Corp. Ltd. -Rs. 22.23	4. Mahatma Phule Backward Class Dev. Corp. -Rs. 98.81		
		12. Mahila Arthik Vikas Mahamandal - Rs. 10.41	5. Vasnatrao Naik Vimukta Jatis and Nomadic Tribes Dev. Corp. Ltd. -Rs. 23.98		
Total for the Department	1(-Rs. 17.61)	3(-Rs. 40.99)	3(-Rs. 133.04)		
G. Irrigation Department			6.Maharashtra Land Dev. Corp. Ltd. -Rs. 152.17		
Total for the Department			1(-Rs. 152.17)		
H. Hoising and Social Assistance Department					3. Maharashtra Housing and Area Dev.

(Contd...)

1	2	3	4	5	6
					Authority -Rs. 368.42
Total for the Department					1(-Rs. 368.42)
I. Medical Education and Drugs Department	13. Haffiki Bio-Pharmaceutical Corp. Ltd.				
Total for the Department	1(+Rs. 96.50)				
J. Reserves and Forests Dep.	14. Forest Dev. Corp. of Maharashtra Ltd. Rs.145.21				
	15. Maharashtra State Farming Corp. Ltd. +Rs. 129.69				
Total for the Department	2(Rs. 274.90)				

(Contd...)

1	2	3	4	5	6
K. Home Department			7 Maharashtra State Police Housing and Welfare Corp. Ltd.		4. Maharashtra State Road Transport Corp. (-Rs. 8986.95)
Total for the Department			1(0)		1(-Rs. 8986.95)
L. Education and Employment Dep.	16. Overseas Employment and Export promotion Corp. of Maharashtra Ltd. (-Rs. 6.38)				
Total for the Department	1(-Rs. 6.38)				
TOTAL	16(Rs. 270.50)	12 (- Rs. 239.60)	7(-Rs. 309.13)	2(Rs.497.31)	4(-Rs. 7693.31)

Annexure – II

State Public Enterprises –
Guidelines for the –

GOVERNMENT OF MAHARASHTRA
Finance Department
Resolution No. PSU- 1088 / CR – 55 / PSU- I
Mantralaya, Bombay – 400 032. Dated 9the December 1989.

RESOLUTION

1. In view of the large financial involvement of the State Government in various State Public Enterprises (PSEs), the necessity of closely monitoring the working of the undertakings has been felt, not only to ensure adequate returns on investments made by the Government in them but also that they function effectively, efficiently and economically while achieving the objective for which the enterprises have been set up. With this end in view, government is now pleased to issue detailed guidelines attached as Annexure to this resolution.

2. These guidelines will be applicable to all the PSEs of the State Government. It is expected that the guidelines will provide a framework for healthy interaction between the enterprises, Administrative Department and the Bureau of State Public Enterprises, leading to speedier and improved decision-making as well as better overall performance of the enterprise.

3. The Administrative Department of Mantralaya are requested to bring these guidelines to the notice of the enterprises, including their subsidiaries, under their administrative control and ensure that they are followed scrupulously.

By order and in the name of the Governor of Maharashtra

Encl.: Annexure.

To

Secretary to Governor
Secretary to Chief Minister
Personal Assistants to all Ministers and Ministers of State

Chief Secretary to Government
Secretaries, all Departments of Mantralaya
Special Commissioner, Maharashtra Sadan, New Delhi
Chief Executives/Managing Directors of all State Public Enterprises
All Desks in Finance Department
(Annexure to Government Resolution, Finance Department, No.PSU-1088/CR-55/PSU-I, Dated December 1989 Regarding Guidelines State Public Enterprises.)

OBJECTIVE

1. A clearer definition of objectives will be a *sin ous non* in any attempt at monitoring and improving the performance of the public enterprises. Thus it is felt that all the enterprises should work to pre-determined long/medium – term (5 years) objectives as well as short- term objectives (annual) which should be set out clearly in both physical and financial terms. The assumptions on which these objectives are based should be formally stated. In stating the enterprises objectives, it will be necessary to be explicit as possible. While some objectives can be directly qualified such as increase in sales, income or return on investment, by some per centage, many other possible objectives such as improvement in service, can be indirectly quantified (e.g., reduced complaints per thousand customers by certain per centage). The ability to assess performance and improve upon it, will be proportional to the clarity with which the objectives are defined.

2. In defining these objectives there should be a clear demarcation between commercial and non- commercial (socio-economic and promotional) objectives. In both the cases, these would be a physical and financial targets. Where the activity is commercial in nature, return's expected from the enterprise should be laid down after being mutually agreed between the enterprises. The Administrative department and the Bureau of State Public Enterprises (BSPE). If the enterprise is required either 'suo moto' or by Government to undertake a promotional activity or to subsidies certain products or service, these would

need to be set out clearly. The losses sustained in such operations should be quantified and explicitly stated and there should be no hidden subsidies. The need for subsidisation of such activities would have to be fully justified and should be made good primarily from surpluses generated by the enterprise form within or through commercial activities, wherever feasible. Subsidisation form Government should be sought only as a last resort. All this pre- supposes that each activity whether commercial or non-commercial, is clearly demarcated. The basic intention in doing this is to bring about transparency in operations so that inefficiencies are not concealed.

3. The long-term objectives should be reviewed once every five years by the department concerned with the public enterprise's top management. The BSPE should be fully involved in these reviews.

4. The annual objectives/operating plans for a financial year should be jointly agreed upon by an enterprise and the department concerned by September of the preceding financial year. Here again, the BSPE should be closely associated with the formulation of these plans.

ROLE OF PUBLIC ENTERPRISES

Government enterprises should not involve themselves in area/activities which can be profitably undertaken by the private sector. Even in respect of current activities of the public enterprises (undertaken initially as a pioneering activity new field), early review should be taken to assess the need for the enterprise to continue with such activities in the light of the subsequent developments e.g. entry of the private sector in such fields, new demands on the resources of the enterprises taking up activities in other fields, profitability of the earlier activities, etc. should such a review so indicate, public enterprises ought to seek to transfer such activities to the public sector, with the approval of the Government. In addition to possibilities of transfering totally unviable activities to the private sector to operate more efficiently in such areas. Basically the intention here is that the resources generated in this way, wether by way of saving of resources or those generated due to effecting transfers to the private sector, may be recycled into areas where the private sector is either shy or precluded form operating.

C. PREPARATION OF PROJECT REPORTS

1. The rationale for corporate structure exists not only in the flexibility in operation and the speed in decision making that it facilitates, but also in the ability to mobilize funds from sources other than the Government. As a consequence, it is essential that project reports are prepared in format, which would enable various enterprises to mobilise financial resources form banks and financial institutions.

2. A project report would comprise the following:

   a. Principle economic and social objectives

   b. Alternative strategic/technologies for achieving these objectives and the rationale for choosing the preferred alternative

   c. Outline of the project

   d. Major assumptions

      i. Market (target, population, volume and price)

      ii. Input costs

      iii. Yield, quality etc. and

   e. Financial data –

      i. Capital structure, sources of funds debt-equity ratio etc. and

      ii. Financial analysis –

1. Item wise capital expenditure
2. Operating costs
3. Income flows

4. Annual profitability projections and cash flows over the project life and
5. Sensivity analysis

ANNUAL REQUIREMENT OF FUNDS

Each enterprise should projects its annual requirement funds in relation to –

a. ongoing/approved projects
b. new projects and
c. subsidies/restructuring of capital

This exercise should be completed for the ensuing the financial year by September end of the preceding year to enable appropriate provisions to be made in the State Budget. Proposals involving expenditure of a "capital" nature should be implemented by a public enterprise after approval by Government. Government approval would also be necessary for incurring expenditure excess of the approved capital outlays for projects and schemes.

REVENUE EXPENDITURE

1. Authorisation of any revenue expenditure towards buying raw materials and paying for services like power, fuel, water can be delegated by the Chief Executive to his Financial Manager as long as the expenses are with in the approved operating plan for the year. A procedure for getting approval for expenditure outside the frame work of the plan should be set out in which the Chief Executive/Board/Government approval is required.

2. A formal procedure and organisation should be set out for placing contracts for equipment, buildings, services etc.. The procedure for tendering, receiving and scrutinising the bids should be clearly spelt out and rigidly followed. If the lowest tender is to be rejected the reasons for so doing should be clearly stated by thè Committee/authority responsible for awarding contracts.

ORGANISATION STRUCTURE AND PERSONNEL POLICIES

1. Organisation structure: the organisation structure of each enterprise should be prepared in a diagrammatic form and updated annually. On the basis of this and the long- term plans of the company, a manpower plan involving recruitment, training and re- training should be drawn up.

2. Delegation of Powers: a document which defines precise responsibility of all employees of the public enterprise form supervisory levels upwards should be prepared and suitable powers to enable this responsibility to be efficiently discharged delegated in writing. This delegation of powers should cover financial authorities and all personnel functions such as appointments, travel, leave, promotion, disciplinary action, transfers etc.. This document should be scrutinised every three years to assess its suitability as also whenever there is a major organisational change or a change in the strategy or future activities of the organisation.

3. Recruitment Policies: the tightest scrutiny is required in regard to any steps which lead to fresh recruitment, approval of the Government should be sought for such recruitment. In fact a detailed review should be conducted with in each enterprise which may bring to light inappropriate mix in the categories of staff in the enterprise. This may necessitate redeployment, after re-training so as to bring the organisational structure and the personnel deployment in line with the organisational objectives and strategies.

4. Terms and conditions and Pay and Allowances: the terms and conditions governing employment of the Directors need also to be reviewed. It is necessary that the terms and conditions of appointment of the Directors on the Board of a public enterprise and avoided. Any change in the scales of pay and allowances of the employees should be made only with the express approvals of the Government. Where the State Government is currently financing part or whole of the staff

cost the enterprise should under a review in order to lessen the burden of such costs on the State Government.

PERFORMANCE EVALUATION

1. In the section of objectives, it has already been stated that there is a need to define performance indicators clearly and set out physical and financial targets for the enterprise as a whole. Having laid down the performance indicators, it would be necessary to monitor and evaluate the performance of the enterprise vis-à-vis these indicators.

2. The performance of each enterprise should be reviewed once in six months by the department concerned. For this purpose, the Annual Plan should be broken up into half-yearly plans. The association of the Bureau would be desirable in such performance reviews and these reviews should be linked to the release of funds, which may be required from the Government. The performance reviews should highlight variance form the budgeted figures both on the receipt and the expenditure side as well as the means to minimize such variances. The performance of the management may be judged on the basis of these reviews.

ACCOUNTING SYSTEMS

The need for a sound accounting system cannot be over emphasized. A sound accounting system involves not only timely compilation and finalisation of accounts but also requires that the data thrown up by the system are authentic and can be used by the management in decision making. It is desirable that the procedure as well as accounts data are set out in a Accounts Manual for each enterprise. It is absolutely essential that accounts are maintained activity-wise and for each unit separately as only such an accounting system would reveal inefficiencies where they exist. It is equally important that the accounts are compiled and finanlised on time. In the absence of timely finalisation of accounts it is not possible to trace the source of adverse financial results and timely corrective action is thus precluded. In this regard it needs to be pointed out that Companies Act 1956 requires all companies to finalize their accounts and obtain approval to the audited accounts within 180 days of the close of the financial/accounting year.

COSTING

In order that an enterprise makes optimum use of the opportunities and resources available, it is necessary to analyze the activities of the enterprise by predetermined cost centers. It is felt that only such a costing systems would highlight areas requiring cost and the appropriate activity/product mix for the enterprise. It is not possible to arrive at the "Least Cost Solution" in the absence of sound cost data.

MANAGEMENT INFORMATION SYSTEM

Each enterprise should set up a Management Information System so that management gets the relevant information required for decision making in key result areas. This system should focus on bringing to the attention of the Chief Executive/ Board the following on a monthly basis:

a.	Monthly Cumulative/ to date Profit and Loss Statement	Compared to budget	Division-wise where possible and relevant
b.	Cash Flow	- do -	- do -
c.	Physical Performance	- do -	- do -
d.	Projection for following month	- do -	- do -

INTERNAL AUDIT

1. A Strong internal audit department reporting directly to the Chief Executive should be set up in each enterprise. A part form checking routine matters like vouchers and physical stock, the emphasis should be to focus attention on corrective practices which –

a. Can lead to wastage or misappropriations

b. Cause delays in getting decisions because of cumbersome procedure

c. Lead to excessive paper work etc.

2. Such an audit team should comprise multi- disciplinary personnel with experience in finance , technical , purchase and marketing functions.

Annexure III

Table 6.3 Statement showing returns in PSEs by category of enterprise

Name of the Enterprise	*Dividends * (% age)*		*Return on # Capital Employed* (% age)		*Return on # Share - holders Equity*		*Profit /Loss (Rs. In Lakh)*	
	1989	1990	1989	1990	1989	1990	1989	1990
Commercial	0.59	0.50	4.21	5.17	0.05	2.59	5.41	270.46
Financial	1.93	0.28	0.74	2.22	5.40	158.44	497.31	
Commercial – cum Promotional	0.15	0.13					-236.99	-239.60
Promotional							-711.80	-309.13
Public Utility							-386.30	-7693.31

* Computed in respect of commercial, financial and commercial –cum promotional enterprises only.

Computed in respect of commercial and financial enterprises only.

7

Outline of Activity of State Public Sector Undertakings in Orrisa*

At present there are 33 Public Sector Undertakings (PSUs) in the State. Out of these 33 Public Sector Undertakings, 5 are statutory Corporations formed under various legislation of state or central government and the rest 28 are registered under the Companies Act. The list of PSUs is at Annexure – I.

These PSUs can be broadly classified into 3 categories viz.: Promotional, Financial and Commercial. While eight Public Sector undertakings come under promotional category and 2 under financial category the rest 23 Public Sector undertakings come under commercial category. The categorization of each Corporation has been indicated in Annexure - 2.

Investment: As on 31st March 1990 the total investment in the Public sector undertakings of the State has been provisionally calculated at Rs. 1769.50 crores, consisting of Rs. 415.85 crores as paid up capital and Rs. 1353.65 crores as term loan. The investment by State Government in form of share capital and term loan amounts to Rs. 391.21 crores and Rs. 431.86 crores constituting 94.1% and 31.9% of the total share capital and loan in these undertakings respectively. The details of

* S.Pradhan, Director-cum-Additional Secretary to Government, Department of Public Enterprises, Government of Orissa, Bhubaneswar.

investment in paid-up capital and term loan is indicated in Annexure – 3.

Table 7.1 The Resources and Utilisation In PSUs

Resource	*Rs. In Crores*	*Utilisation*	*Rs. In crores*
Share Capital	364.26	Gross Fixed Assets	1449.35
Term Loan	1341.43	Investment	441.19
Internal Sources	459.15	Current Assets	800.50
Current Liability	742.16	Intangible Assets including	
Miscellaneous	146.31	Accumulated loss	314.74
		Miscellaneous	47.53
	3053.31		3053.31

Table 7.2 Top Five PSUs in Investment

Sl. No.	*Name of the PSUs*	*Investment as on*	
		31.03.90	*31.03.89*
1.	Orissa State Electricity Board	333.82	218.98
2.	Orissa Power Generation Corp.	61.70	36.17
3.	Industrial Promotion &Investment Corp.	61.27	52.97
4.	Industrial Devl. Corp.	54.15	53.15
5.	Orissa Lift Irrigation Corp.	51.46	45.07
		562.40	406.34

Turnover of Production and Services

Table 7.3 Turnover of PSUs (1987-88 to 1989-90)

Year	*Turnover*		
	Manufacturing Enterprises	*Service Enterprises*	*Total*
1987-88	600.52	425.62	1026.14
1988-89	685.44	534.50	1219.94
1989-90	830.23	493.39	1323.62

Employment

The PSUs play an important role in removing the unemployment problem in the State. Besides indirect employment these undertakings have given direct employment ti 85,417 persons up to end of 1989-90. The break-up of the employment is as below:

i.	Managerial Supervisory and others	14,606
ii.	Workmen & Others	70,811
iii.	Total	85,417

Government SLPE relation

The State Government have created a new Department – the Department of Public Enterprises on 4th January, 1991 to function as the nodal department to oversee and regulate the functioning of PSUs in the State. This new Department have been entrusted with the task of laying down general policies and guidelines for the effective management of PSUs, regulating the industrial project proposals of the PSUs through project approval committee of the State Government, prescribing norms of financial discipline budgeting accounting and audit of PSUs detecting sickness in PSUs and advise measures against their sickness and prescribing model Memorandum of Understanding (MOUs) etc.

With a view to closely monitor the activities of the PSUs and to take part in the decision making process of the PSUs. The State Government have nominated official directors form the Department of Public Enterprises and from the finance department to the Boards of each PSUs in the State. The duty of these nominee official directors is to report to the Government of any mismanagement in PSUs so as to enable Government to take immediate remedial measures. This would now enable Government to keep vigil on the day to day decision making of the PSUs.

New Development in the Government SLPE interface monitoring mechanism

The state Government have initiated action for entering into MOU with PSUs to improve their performance by giving them operational and mission for the Corporation to be achieved. The advantage of the system is to make the PSUs more effective and efficient by charting priorities and by providing clear direction for growth and achievement. To begin with, Government have asked six corporations Viz.

1. Orissa Industrial Development Corporation
2. Orissa Mining Corporation
3. Orissa Agro Industries Corporation
4. Orissa Power Generation Corporation
5. Konark Televisions Ltd. and
6. Orissa State Electronics Development Corporation to submit the MOU to Government for approval by end of February 1992.

In order to make the Corporation viable, the State Government have proposed to merge PSUs having similar activities and operating in the same line of business. The Orissa State Road Transport Company has been amalgamated with Orissa State Road Transport Corporation and Orissa Plantation Development Corporation and Similiphar Forest Development Corporation have been merged with Orissa Forest Development Corporation. Proposals are now under consideration for merger of Orissa Police Housing and Welfare Corporation with Orissa State Housing Board both of which are engaged in civil construction activities.

The State Government have directed the PSUs to formulate Corporate Planning indicating their long terms goals which could be dovetailed into the Five Year Plan of the State and to make annual action plan to achieve their objectives envisaged in their Corporate Plan. The main objective of the Corporate Plan exercise is to make the functioning of the PSUs more target oriented.

Constraints being faced by Government Corporations in Orissa in their functioning

In my view the following constraints are being faced by the Government Corporations which hampers efficient functioning

1. Lack of Personnel Policy
2. Lack of Functional autonomy
3. Lack of proper Infrastructure facilities
4. Weakness of Marketing set up
5. Weakness of Capital base
6. Lack of Accountability

Most of the Government Corporations in Orissa lacked proper personnel policy. Very few had any professional Management cadre to man the Corporations. Most of the Management cadre lacked in commitment towards professionalism due to various factors.

To over come this problem the personnel who would man the management cadre and higher echelon of the Corporations should be properly selected after extensive talent search. In the Indian context it is important that the personnel who are selected to head the organizations could make or mar the organisation. Therefore, the persons who are selected to head the Corporations should not only be professionals but should be technically equipped to head the organisation.

Without exception, most of the Corporation lacked functional autonomy. Government should strive to select proper persons to head the Corporation. But once they are selected complete autonomy should be accorded to them to function in business like manner within the parameters laid down by Government for the operation of the Corporations. Unless and until autonomy devolves upon the Corporation a sense of responsibility will be lacking. To overcome this the Government can start entering into MOU with the corporation laying down targets and achievement for the year. Once targets are laid down Government should avoid interfering in the day to day functioning. It should extend all possible backing for achieving the targets.

Some of the corporations who have manufacturing units lack some basic infrastructure facilities like Telecommunication and Banking. In 1990's communication is of primordial importance. Unless and until there is complete flow of information between the head office and the manufacture units, decisions taking will be delayed which affects the overall functioning of the Corporations. If possible the major manufacturing units should have personal computer based fax and telex system. Banks should be requested to open branches with Mercantile divisions functioning in these places.

Unless and until proper reports are submitted in time to the head office there would be no control on accounts and also manufacturing operations. My experience shows that most of the accounts finalizations are delayed by more than 4-5 years. The head office in most cases was not in a position to know the operational situation in the field. The balance sheet of the corporation is the mirror through which one can know the health of the Corporation. But seldom any corporation had up to date Balance Sheet. In reality the head Office were doing post mortem of the Corporations finance and in some case manufacturing operations. In fact the corporation head office should be doing corporate planning for the future and laying down targets and monitoring.

Some of the corporations in Orissa lack proper Marketing set up in their functioning. Unless and until the product, which is produced or manufactured, is marketed with remunerative price the corporations profit and health will be severely jeopradized. Unfortunately some of the corporations lack the proper marketing studies, very few research units have been set up to study the market and take necessary preventive steps in improving the bottom line.

Orissa has substantial mineral deposits. But unfortunately we do not have any research set up which would forecast the world trend of demand and supply positions for important areas in the next 10 to 15 years including taking care of the market fluctuation. The manufacturing and trading units should have proper marketing set up to guide the functioning of all the important corporations. Marketing is a vital aspect of any company's functioning one might produce goods, but without super marketing, the company could be saddled with heavy stock of inventory and unsold goods which will ultimately affect the health of the company.

Most of the corporations have been set up with very weak capital base. I am of the view that some of the corporations, which have overlapping functioning, should wind up or merged. By this recurring expenditure would be avoided.

If a corporation is set up it is the duty of the Government to take proper care in nursing the organisation till it bears fruits. For this Government should allow enough funding and financial autonomy, so that it does not function as an appendix of the Government Departments. Obviously, a difference must be made between a corporation and Department of Government.

Unless and until the Corporation receives proper financial help from Government they will not be in a position to deliver the goods. One of the reasons some corporations have become sick is mainly for their weak capital base.

Accountability should be fixed. The managers in Government Corporation are nothing but trustees of the Government. If the organisation has not functioned properly then there should be surgical operations to remove the tumour in time. Unless and until accountability is fixed nobody will be willing to deliver the goods. These will be passing of the bulk. Some of the corporations which I had assessed lacked accountability for which Government has lost substantial money. Once accountability is fixed efficiency should improve.

It is no doubt that some of the Government Corporations have done Yeoman Services in developing the States Industrial and infrastructure bases. They have also undertaken lot of social service in opening the hinterland. It is a fact that the business houses 'ould not have gone to some of the areas where the Corporations have installed their industrial units. Along with this social accountability, financial accountability must be ensured.

Views of the Author

The 33 Corporations in Orissa could be categorized into 4 categories.

1. Those which are done well and are able to generate their own resources.
2. Those which are basically strong but are making losses
3. One's which are continuously losing and whose viability is in question.
4. One's which are in the implementation stage.

In category – I there are 7 Corporations. In category –2 there are 9 Corporations. It has been seen that the corporations in category – 3 have never made profits since their inception and according to me there is very little scope for them to make profit. The 16 Corporations, which are in Category – 3 have eroded their capital. Their net worth is negative. But unfortunately some of them are in public utility service like road transport. Obviously it will be politically impossible to close down or privatise the Transport Corporation. Recently Dr. A.V.Raman, an expert form Central Institute of Road Transport, Pune has joined Orissa State Road Transport Corporation on deputation as F.A. – cum- Chief Accounts Officer. With the help of Dr. Raman the mission and Objectives of the Corporation are being clearly specified and we are hopeful that the loss which is to the tune of Rs. 1 crore every month will be reduced by about 50% with the steps which have been initiated after his joining.

The other Corporations in category – 3 are being closely watched and still no decision have been taken on the action to be taken. According to me, putting them in the joint sector could make some adjustments or some of them could be merged with other Corporations to make the viable. I would personally go in for liquidation of some corporation. I am of future view that Government should not patronize activities, which could be better done by private sectors and fritter away scare resources like manufacturing of shoes, textiles etc.

Chief Minister of the state has clearly directed that unless and until the corporations, which are losing, must turn round in next 2 years. If this is not done than he is willing to sell them or Government is agreeable to hand over the employees to run them.

I am of the view that some of the Corporations should immediately be privatised to stop further financial hemorrhage years after year and the Government should restrict itself to patronizing few corporations which are of prime importance for the infrastructural development of the States. Orissa is a mineral rich state and if proper infrastructure development such as road, communication etc. is done by the Corporations under the State Government control this will have multiplier effect and lead to rapid industrialization of the mineral sector at least. Orissa Government could develop this mineral based Corporations, so that the return on investment in quick and fast. Orissa Mining Corporation that is the premier mineral-based corporation of the state is likely to disclose profit of about Rs. 30 crores during 1991-92. This corporation is mainly dealing with iron ores, manganese and chromite. I am of the further view that some other Corporations should be established to look after minor minerals and which are in abundant supply in the State. Recently, Government has sold the loss-making unit of Orissa Mining Corporation - charge chrome plant to TISCO. TISCO has taken over both the assets and liabilities of the charge chrome plant. The liability fare outweighed the assets. Fortunately, some of the mineral-based plants run by Orissa Government Corporation are doing well like KIW, Barbil and Cement Plant at Baragarh.

Finally, I am of the view that there has to be a case by case approach to each Corporations needs and wants and the action to be formulated in each case.

Annexure – I

List of Public Sector Undertakings

Sl.No.	*Name of the Public Sector Undertakings*
1.	2.
	Statutory Corporations
1.	Orissa State Electricity Board, Bhubaneswar
2.	Orissa State Warehousing Corporation, Bhubaneswar
3.	Orissa State Road Transport Corporation, Cuttack
4.	Orissa State Financial Corporation, Cuttack
5.	Orissa Industrial Infrastructure Development Corporation, Bhubaneswar
	Government Companies
6.	Orissa Lift Irrigation Corporation Ltd., Bhubaneswar
7.	Orissa Mining Corporation Ltd., Bhubaneswar
8.	Industrial Promotion and Investment Corporation of Orissa Ltd., Bhubaneswar
9.	Orissa State Handloom Development Corporation Ltd.
10.	Orissa Small Industries Corporation Ltd., Cuttak
11.	Orissa Maritime and Chilka Area Development Corporation Ltd.
12.	Orissa Hills Development Corporation Ltd., Cuttak
13.	Orissa Construction Corporation, Bhubaneswar
14.	Orissa State Leather Corporation, Cuttak
15.	Orissa Fish Food Development Corporation Ltd, Bhubaneswar
16.	Orissa Tourism Development Corporation Ltd., Bhubaneswar
17.	Orissa State Civil Supplies Corporation Ltd. Bhubaneswar
18.	Orissa Police Housing & Welfare Corporation Ltd., Bhubanewar
19.	Orissa Cashew Development Corporation Ltd., Bhubaneswar
20.	Orissa Agro Industries Corporation Ltd.

Categorisation of Undertaking

Promotional	*Financial*	*Commercial*
1. Orissa Film Dev. Corp.	1. Orissa State Fin. Corp.	1. Orissa State Warehousing Corp. Ltd.
2. Orissa Handloom Dev. Corp.	2. IPICOL	2. Orissa State Electricity Board
3. Orissa State Seeds Corp.		3. Orissa State Road Transport Corp.
4. Orissa Tourism Dev. Corp.		4. IDCO
5. Orissa Fish Seed Dev. Corp.		5. Orissa Mining Corp.
6. Orissa State Electronic Dev. Corp.		6. Orissa Agro. Ind. Corp.
7. Orissa Lift irrigation Corp.		7. Orissa Constructing Corp.
		8. Orissa State Export Dev. Corp
		9. IDC
		10. Orissa State Commercial Transport Corp.
		11. Orissa State Leather Corp.
		12. New Mayurbhanj Textiles

(Contd...)

13. Orissa Maritime and Chilka Area Development Corp.
14. Orissa State Cashew Deve. Corp.
15. Orissa Police Housing and Welfare Corp.
16. Orissa Civil Supplies Corp.
17. Orissa State Textile Corp.
18. Konark TV Ltd.
19. Orissa Bridge and Construction Corp.
20. Orissa Power Generating Corp.
21. Orissa Textile Mills
22. Orissa Small Industries Corp.
23. Orissa Instruments Co.

8

Privatisation and Non-Privatisation Reforms in State Level Public Enterprises: Sectorwise Strategy and Implications*

The paper proposes to discuss the sectorwise strategy and implications of privatisation and non-privatisation reforms in the State Level Public Enterprises (SLPEs). As a backdrop, it provides the profile and classification of these enterprises.

Profiles of SLPEs

The SLPEs, as instrument of public policy to accelerate the pace of development naturally proliferated very quickly. About 90 per cent of the 754 SLPEs were set up through the Third to Sixth five year Plans. The years 1980-81 to 1986-87 have seen the setting up of a maximum number of 350 SPLEs.

Annexure-1 shows the growth of the SLPEs state-wise during the Plan period. These enterprises have been organized under a variety of legal structures such as departmental undertakings, statutory corporations and boards, government

---

* SLPEs Working Group, Institute of Public Enterprise, Osmania University Campus, Hyderabad-500 007

companies, cooperative societies and joint sector companies. Almost 75 per cent of these enterprises have been organized as government companies under the Companies Act. About 15 per cent of these enterprises were incorporated as statutory boards or commissions. The departmental enterprises constitute less than 10 per cent of total number of these enterprises. The cooperative enterprises do not form part of this study as many states do not form part of this study as many states do not treat them as part of the SLPEs system. The investment in these enterprises excluding the state electricity boards and the state road transport corporations was Rs. 2060 crores as on March 31, 1997. This rose to over Rs. 13000 crores as on March 31,1987. The investments in the SLPEs grew on an average at the rate of 45 per cent per annum during the period 1976-77 to 1986-87 in the case of the SLPEs as compared to 30 per cent per annum in the case of CPEs during the same period.

Annexure-2 gives the state-wise investment pattern from 1981-82 to 1986-87 for the SLPEs.

The debt-equity ration heavily leaned in favour of the equity components. In very few states such as Kerala and West Bengal the debt component assumed higher proportions mainly due to accumulated losses as the losses were usually founded by debt advances made by the concerned state governments to these enterprises.

The SLPEs across the various states were characterized by a low productivity of investments therein. For all the states taken together, the asset turnover ratio was 3:2:1 as on March 31, 1987 , indicating that per rupee of investment the turnover, i.e. goods and services sold, was only about 31 paise in these enterprises. Financially, these enterprises did not measure up to expectations. The gross and operating margins in these enterprises were not adequate enough to yield desirable level of net profits after providing for financial charges and taxes. About forty per cent of these enterprises were in the red at the gross margin level and another fifty per cent incurred losses at the operating margin level leaving about ten per cent of the enterprise showing small surpluses.

Annexure-3 shows the financial performance of the SLPEs during the periods of the study in terms of profit after taxes. The internal resources generated by these enterprises have been measured in terms of retained earnings plus depreciation and deferred revenue expenditure. The performance of the SLPEs not encouraging with regard to the generation of the internal resources from 1981-82 to 1986-87.

Annexure- 4 shows that during this period for all the enterprises taken together for all the states, the internal resources generation was negative. However, in 1986-87 these enterprises broke away form the past by generating Rs. 43 crores as internal resources. This constituted less than .5 per cent of the Capital investment in these enterprises during the year. The study of the 'net-worth' in these enterprises points out that the SLPEs on the whole had accumulated losses. The extent of accumulated losses to paid-up capital increased from 24 per cent in 1980-81 to 39 per cent in 1986-87 for all the SLPEs taken together. The increase was faster in the case of States such as Bihar, Himachal Pradesh, Rajasthan and Tripura.

Annexure –5 depicts the accumulated losses as per centage of paid up capital in the SLPEs. It is relevant to mention here that the financial position of the SLPEs was influenced by the top ten profit leaders and an equal number of loss-makers.

Annexure-6 shows that as between the two kinds of the SLPEs the losses accumulated by the latter were ten times (say Rs.760 crores) mare than the total profits earned by the former (say Rs. 76 crores) in 1986-87.

Classification

These enterprises are engaged in a wide spectrum of activities including industrial development and financial promotion, trading and marketing, contract and construction, consumer and engineering goods, development of backward regions upliftment of weaker sections of the society, Agro-industrial production, mining of minerals and metals, development of small industries and tourism. For the purpose of this paper, the SLPEs have been grouped under five broad categories as follows:

1. Manufacturing enterprises
2. Trading and Service enterprises
3. Financial enterprises
4. Promotional and Developmental enterprises and
5. Welfare enterprises.

It may be noted that these categories have been so arranged that as we go down the listing, the commercial objectives become less important and social objectives get greater emphasis. As on March 31, 1987 there were 250 manufacturing, 121 trading and service, 54 financial, 236 promotional and 93 welfare SLPEs in the country.

Annexure – 8 shows the distribution of the SLPEs in terms of the five categories. The relative importance of the various kinds of SLPEs differed from state to state with reference to their economic strategy. For example, West Bengal and Kerala set up more of manufacturing enterprises in view of the commitment of left oriented governments to control the productive activities. As opposed to this, the states such as Maharashtra, Gujarat and Tamil Nadu had more number of financial and promotional enterprises because of their strategy to accelerate the pace of economic development through helping the private enterprises. In the states such as Uttar Pradesh, Bihar and Madhya Pradesh the accent was more on setting up area development corporations as the intra-regional imbalances were a major issue in these states.

Role and Relevance of Sectoral Activities

We have already seen the macro objectives and the classification matrix of the SLPEs. In this section we will examine the relevance of the continuation of the existing activities belonging to the five categories of the SLPEs.

Manufacturing State Level Public Enterprises (MSLPEs)

These enterprises constitute about one-third of the SLPEs portfolio. In some states they contribute a major share of the total SLPEs portfolio. These states include Assam, Gujarat, Kerala, Maharastra, Rajasthan, Tamil Nadu, Uttar Pradesh and West Bengal in terms of capital investment. The MSLPEs had an investment of more investment of more than 25 per cent of the total investment in the SLPEs.

Annexure-9 reveals that Andhra Pradesh, Assam, Bihar, Gujarat, Jammu & Kashmir, Karnataka, Kerala, Maharashtra, Orissa, Tamil Nadu, Uttar Pradesh and West Bengal had relatively higher investments in these enterprise. The physical and financial performance of these enterprises show that their capacity utilisation ranged from 25 to 50 per cent in most of the states. The financial performance of these enterprises has become very important in view of the budgetary deficit of the state governments. Against 12 per cent of profits before interest and taxes (PBIT) on capital invested, the rate of return, shown by Annexure -10, fluctuated between -.053 per cent in 1981-82 to 3.72 per cent in 1986-87 for the SLPEs taken together as a whole.

The MSLPEs have been set up for filling up the entrepreneurial gap in the private sector in the various states and undertaking capital intensive and risk-prone industrial activity. They have also been set up for exploiting the technological advantage in favour of the states in the areas of high-tech base, operating the monopoly business and for generating surpluses for the planned development of the states. It is also noteworthy that a considerable number of these enterprises are taken-over sick units. As shown by Annexure - 11 the product - range of these enterprises is widely diversified form soaps, detergents, sericulture, paper, mining, cement and sugar units to light and heavy engineering, steel and scooters.

A review of their objectives raises a number of issues. When these enterprises taken as a whole have been incurring losses year after year why should they be retained in the SLPEs portfolio? Should any SLPE operate as a monopoly business? Why should state governments create competition for the private sector units by setting up enterprises on their own as there are number of other ways to encourage competition for and within the private sector? Why should state governments fill up the entrepreneurship gap instead of promoting the entrepreneurial culture? Why should state government continue to run the small sized MSLPEs which could well be run by the private sector entrepreneurs?

Viewed from the product portfolio of these enterprises, there cannot be a strong defence built up in favour retaining the manufacturing of soaps, detergents, scooters, textiles, cements and light industrial items. The paper and mining industries get qualified by this norm for retention in the SLPEs portfolio. We may go a step further and even suggest the need for turningover the high-tech MSLPEs to the private sector as by that time sufficient private incentive should be able to forehead to take over such activities from the public sector. The acceptance of this suggestion may free funds to the tune of about 3000 crores form the MSLPEs and reduction of losses to be born by the state governments of Rs.100 crores per annum.

Trading and Service State Level Public Enterprises (TSLPEs)

These enterprises include marketing, trading and service SLPEs. The state marketing corporations, and state civil supplies and essential commodities supply corporations fall under the mould of this category. Their main objectives vary form marketing of goods produced by small producers undertaking production perishable and durable consumable items, strengthening economics base of producers by providing financial assistance, modernizing their production organisation and marketing of their products to achieving economy in execution of construction works. There were 121 such enterprises with a capital investment of Rs.1588 crores as on March 31, 1987. Their capital investment doubled over the period 1981-82 to 1986-87. In terms of numerical strength Kerala,

Bihar and Karnataka have these enterprises in two digit numbers. In terms of investment in three digit numbers, Punjab was followed by Haryana, Bihar, Karnataka, Uttar Pradesh and Kerala (See: Annexure-12). Against 10 per cent of PBIT on the capital invested the rate of return was hovering around 8.32 per cent in 1986-87 and it was as low as 1.61 per cent in 1983-84 to these states. In fact Bihar, Maharashtra and Tamil Nadu earned the distinction of earning a negative rate of return although during the period 1981-82 to 1986-87 in this category of enterprises (See: Annexure -13). These enterprises had a very low turnover to capital employed ratio. The approach followed in this regard related more to selling then marketing. Most of these enterprises suffered from the glaring incidents of bad cash management. The lingering and increasing overdues and the low working capital turnover support this contention. The cost consciousness was lacking in this set of enterprises. Their pricing policies did not bear the desired relationship to costs. The accumulated losses in these enterprises had eaten away a good chunk of the paid up capital. The handlooms and handicrafts units in the SLPEs had very low physical achievements, especially in the area of modernization of looms. They did not export the targeted amount of cotton fabrics although they had a very high export potential. The construction enterprises as a constituent of the TSLPEs were relegated to the status of mere intermediaries as most of these enterprises worked behind the schedules with respect to various contracts. The civil supplies and essential supply corporations were characterized by laxity in procurement and distribution and incurred an extra expenditure on wasteful item leading to losses. In fact there have been cases when these enterprises embarked upon the schemes without working out their economics and without having any expertise in the connected areas. The off-season procurement were made and the style pursued in obtaining the supplies did not reflect commercial poderence on their part. However, it may be admitted here that these corporations are fulfilling a major social objectives of mitigating food grains shortages in the areas faced with scarcity and providing price-support to agriculturists. It may be difficult to withdraw from this area at this stage. Neverthless, it will be worthwhile to suggest that these enterprises can hive-off the non-food grains procurement activity such as the maintenance of large fleet of trucks, etc. The state warehousing corporations also need to rethink about the relevance of their activities in the present context. It is worth noting that large storage capacities are being developed in the private sector.

The construction corporations incur time and cost overruns disqualify their continuation furthermore as state corporations. As today there is sufficient private expertise and initiative available on this front which can easily substitute for the public economic initiative. The construction activity should be hived off the public sector. Though it is advisable to operate the Handlooms and Handicrafts Corporation in the state sector the export of their products and internal marketing can better be left to the private sector in view of the quick decisional requirements as the basic characteristics of such an activity.

The state trading organisations have lost the golss during the last decade. They have failed to overcome the market failures in order to help the small producers or consumers and are characterized by high rent extractions due to the monopoly in their trading and wind falls of market fluctuation. Most of the state trading organisations has very little freedom in the following market trends and taking up entrepreneurial decisions to promote trade either within the country or outside. Their contribution in the total foreign trade is very insignificant.

Financial State Level Public Enterprises (FSLPEs)

These enterprises include in their ambit the state financial corporations, state industrial development corporations, state investment enterprises, state leasing companies, chit funds and banks and institutions for financing the panchayat raj bodies. They are involved in accelerating the rate of industrialization in the states, removing regional imbalances and promoting growth of tiny, medium and small industries. There were 54 such enterprises with a capital investment of Rs. 5055 crores as on March 31, 1987. Annexure - 14 points out that Maharashtra had a maximum investment of Rs 831 crores in these enterprises followed by Rs. 616 crores in Uttar Pradesh, Rs. 480 crores in Tamil Nadu, Rs. 454 crores in Gujarat and Rs 437 crores in Andhra Pradesh. One- third of the units promoted by these corporations have fallen sick. The disbursement are about 50 per cent of the sanctions in these enterprises. In the case of many such corporations developed regions have received more assistance than the backward regions. They are working mostly as extended arm of the Industrial Development Bank of India engaged in refinancing . Against 9 per cent of the PBIT on capital invested in the years between 1981-82 and 1986-87, as shown by Annexure –15 ; their earnings could not exceed 3.29 per cent in any year of the study. Though these enterprises will have to play a great role in the development process, they will have to introduce fundamental changes in their orientation and working. For instance, they will have to formulate speedy disbursement policies to enable them to be eligible for receiving refinance form the Industrial Development Bank of India on their own without approaching the state governments time and again for the renewed equity support. They will have to innovate new schemes keeping in view their clientele. Similarly, considerable effort will have to be made to step up the recovery of overdues. Instead of expanding their work force and depending in toto on there own personnel they will do well to obtain non-essential services from external agencies.

Promotional State Level Public Enterprises (PSLPEs)

The PSLPEs include the forest development corporations, small-scale industrial development corporations and tourism development corporations and fisheries development corporations. These enterprises are charged with the responsibility of undertaking the activities assigned to them on promotional basis with both non-commercial and commercial objectives. The small-scale industrial development corporations were initiated in the 1960s to help the small-scale industrialists in terms of supply of raw materials, financial inputs and marketing assistance. These enterprises also take up the manufacture of certain products incidental to their main activities. The forest development enterprises were started in the middle of the 1970s. They have been set up to promote social forestry, conserve and commercially exploit forest produce, develop forest wealth and protect the interests of tribal population living in the forest. The tourism development enterprises also sprung up in the 1970s. Almost all the states in the country have tourism development corporations now. These are engaged in promoting tourism in their respective states by helping private entrepreneurs and taking up many schemes on their own. The fisheries development corporations were set up in the 1960s to help the fishermen engaged in selling fish and allied produce. These enterprises have taken up the manufacture of boats, etc. for the fishermen. In nutshell, the PSLPEs primarily undertake the non-commercial functions and in the pursuit to do so they have taken up commercial activities to fulfil the role assigned to them through encouraging the private entrepreneurs by direct involvement, acting as nodal agencies in their area of operations charged with the responsibility of preparing and implementing the plans for the development of respective activities assigned to them, and continuing to function on a self-sustained basis. As on March 31, 1987 there were 248 promotional enterprises followed by 20 in West Bengal, 19 each in Karnataka and Kerala , 17 each in Andhra Pradesh and Tamil Nadu and 16 each in Gujarat and Bihar.

Annexure –16 shows that Andhra Pradesh had a maximum investment of Rs. 263 crores in these enterprises in 1986-87 followed by Rs. 220 crores in Bihar, Rs. 188 crores in Maharashtra and Rs. 157 crores in Orissa. The financial performance of these enterprises was not very promising. Annexure – 17 reveals that their PBIT on capital invested fluctuated between .31 per cent in 1981-82 and 1.43 per cent in 1986-87 against the 8 per cent norm for such enterprises. The SPLEs in Bihar , Manipur, Punjab, and Meghalaya had a minus PBIT during the period 1981-82 to 1986-87. The future course of reform apperars to make them industry-wise councils, where private sector and government can co-operate and undertake promotion efforts. The industry organisations like Confederation of Engineering Industries (CEI), provide a good model.

Welfare State Level Public Enterprises (WSLPEs)

These enterprises are late entrants on the SLPEs scene. Some of these enterprises were set up for the first time during the middle of 1970s by a couple of state governments. However, by the middle of 1980s most of the states of the India Union had established these enterprises. The term WSLPEs is omnibus in its nature and difficult to define. In its wider sense, it includes all such enterprises that are engaged in the welfare of masses of country in general. In the restricted sense of the term, it includes only those enterprises, which are involved in the upliftment of the scheduled castes and scheduled tribes only. However, for the purpose of this paper the WSLPEs may be said to include the schedule castes development enterprises, scheduled tribe development enterprises, minority development enterprises, backward class development enterprises and area development enterprise. These enterprises have not been set up under a specific form of organisation, a survey of the practices prevailing in different states shows that these enterprises have been established either as the Government companies, or co-operative societies or statutory corporations, form a mere 11 in 1975-76 the number of WSLPEs shot up to 82 in 1986-87. Of the 82 WSLPEs, 50 are functioning in 13 States as scheduled castes and scheduled tribe, women development and minorities enterprises. The rest of the 32 were scattered over 8 states as area development enterprises and have been incorporated in the form of Government companies. There is no uniformity in the distribution of these enterprises across the states. Uttar Pradesh had a maximum of 16 WSLPEs followed by 12 in Maharashtra, 11 in Madhya Pradesh and 10 in Kerala. The WSLPEs were conspicuous by their absence in Goa, Jammu and Kashmir, Himachal Pradesh, West Bengal,

Meghalaya and Orissa. The broad objectives of these enterprises relate to helping the weaker sections of the society to enable them of cross poverty line through a gradual and sustained effort, transforming the economic structure of the weaker sections through the entrepreneurial mode, working for the social upliftment of down trodden strata of the society through working for their educational upsurge, and mobilizing the institutional credit for the socio-economic upliftment of the weaker sections of the society. Annexure-18 shows that the WSLPEs had an investment of Rs. 471 crores in 1986-87. Uttar Pradesh, Andhra Pradesh Gujarat and Maharashtra had a lion's share in the investment of these enterprises. These enterprises have been although in the red for all the states taken together during the period 1981-82 to 1986-87. Against the norm of 5 per cent PBIT on capital invested. Annexure –19 shows that only Andhra Pradesh, Gujarat, Kerala and Maharashtra could keep head above the water. These corporations were set up to takeover the departmental activities of the state governments with the view that their conversion into corporate enterprises would help in providing such activities the commercial orientation. But the performance of these enterprises has betrayed the hopes. The overheads in these corporations were exorbitantly high. Many schemes did not register much progress. The disbursement per beneficiery / scheme was very low. The margin money advanced was not distributed fully. In a given year the recovery of principal and interest has been very low. Further, they were characterised by organisation structures inconsistent with their objectives. Most of these enterprises suffered form the short tenure of managing directors. In the case of the Andhra Pradesh Scheduled Castes Co-operative Finance Corporations in 1988-89 six Managing Directors were replaced wothin an average tenure of about two months. Most of the general managers and middle level managers were deputationists form government departments with very little corporate understanding. The schemes introduced in a particular year were discontinued very soon. A question may be raised as to why these corporations cannot remove the overlap in their functions and provide better services at reduced costs by curbing down overheads through restructuring. It is worth examinig here as to why these corporations should not be reconverted back into government departments in order to bring down the overheads and to ensure coordination. Since development of weaker sections of society will continue to remain an important concern in years to come, these corporations are expected to play a greater role in case they are not reconverted into government departments. The WSLPEs can grow by leaps and bounds and can acquire in that process the requisite commercial tinge if they mobilise considerable finances from the financial institutions.

Annexure-1

Growth of State Level Public Enterprises During Five Year Plans

S.No.	State	I	II	III	IV	V	VI	VII	Total
1	Andhra Pradesh	3	6	6	7	6	6	2	36
2	Arunachal Pradesh	0	0	0	0	2	1	0	3
3	Assam	3	5	9	9	7	10	0	43
4	Bihar	0	3	5	13	17	7	2	47
5	Goa	0	0	0	0	2	3	2	7
6	Gujarat	0	0	6	10	19	13	0	48
7	Haryana	0	0	1	6	6	6	3	22
8	Himachal Pradesh	0	1	1	2	7	.6	0	17
9	Jammu & Kishmir	2	0	2	5	6	1	0	16
10	Karnataka	7	5	9	15	13	9	0	58
11	Kerala	3	4	14	23	28	15	3	90
12	Madhya Pradesh	1	0	5	9	8	9	0	32
13	Maharashtra	1	4	13	12	11	7	3	51

(Contd...)

14	Manipur	0	0	0	2	2	3	1	8
15	Meghalaya	0	0	0	2	3	3	1	9
16	Misoram	0	0	0	0	0	1	2	3
17	Nagaland	0	0	1	2	1	1	0	5
18	Orissa	3	3	4	3	11	8	1	33
19	Punjab	0	3	3	6	6	5	2	25
20	Rajasthan	1	6	6	7	8	8	0	36
21	Tamil Nadu	1	4	8	9	10	10	2	44
22	Tripura	0	0	0	1	3	2	1	7
23	Utter Pradesh	6	6	10	14	11	10	4	61
24	West Bengal	1	3	6	11	18	14	0	53

Source: data bank on SLPEs, Institute of Public enterprise, Hyd.

Annexure-2

Capital Investment in SLPEs

(Rs. In crores)

S.NO.	State	81-82	82-83	83-84	84-85	85-86	86-87
1	Andhra Pradesh	626	770	982	1,077	1,168	1,364
2	Arunachal Pradesh	4	4	5	5	5	7
3	Assam	101	130	148	186	220	271
4	Bihar	93	129	315	441	538	661
5	Goa	22	25	29	32	35	40
6	Gujarat	338	410	467	534	623	735
7	Haryana	213	234	256	286	314	370
8	Himachal Pradesh	72	78	92	104	111	124
9	Jammu & Kishmir	91	105	128	154	176	204
10	Karnataka	705	795	874	952	1,072	1,238
11	Kerala	482	568	659	736	816	879
12	Madhya Pradesh	216	231	254	289	295	361
13	Maharashtra	808	838	766	920	1,072	1,199

(Contd...)

14	Manipur	7	8	9	10	11	12
15	Meghalaya	19	21	23	26	28	32
16	Misoram	5	5	6	7	8	9
17	Nagaland	14	16	17	18	21	23
18	Orissa	261	314	399	454	519	555
19	Punjab	429	479	545	589	672	749
20	Rajasthan	297	360	422	476	545	607
21	Tamil Nadu	523	567	824	904	981	1,058
22	Tripura	15	17	18	19.00	22	26
23	Utter Pradesh	415	761	916	1,114	1,308	1,535
24	West Bengal	1,322	449	519	588	646	724
	Total	7,078	7,314	8,673	9,921	11,206	12,783

Source: Data bank on SLPEs, Institute of Public enterprise, Hyd.

Annexure-3

Financial Performance of SLPEs

(Profit After Tax in RS.Lakhs)

S.NO.	*State*	*81-82*	*82-83*	*83-84*	*84-85*	*85-86*	*86-87*
1	Andhra Pradesh	535	-3,006	-5,751	-3,680	4,660	4,260
2	Arunachal Pradesh	-80	-30	95	130	105	155
3	Assam	-606	423	-312	-762	-1,904	-1,501
4	Bihar	-1,195	-1,167	-117	-1,234	-1,182	-1,194
5	Goa	8	22	30	28	14	21
6	Gujarat	-558	-1	214	-230	-944	-944
7	Haryana	-51	-188	-317	-234	-198	-762
8	Himachal Pradesh	-35	-17	-29	-6	-12	-12
9	Jammu & Kishmir	54	-60	-55	-230	-346	-154
10	Karnataka	10	10	-19	-18	-14	-577
11	Kerala	-357	-1,747	2,105	-4,662	-5,049	-4,835
12	Madhya Pradesh	-138	-196	-188	-183	-131	516
13	Maharashtra	322	66	-1,168	-1,163	458	0

(Contd...)

14	Manipur	-8	3	-10	-3	-5	9
15	Meghalaya	-45	-60	-38	-13	-65	-53
16	Misoram	0	0	0	0	0	0
17	Nagaland	-15	-28	-35	-41	-10	-28
18	Orissa	-838	257	-309	-660	-31	100
19	Punjab	0	0	0	0	0	0
20	Rajasthan	288	278	-860	-1,250	-1,275	-701
21	Tamil Nadu	53	-5,791	-4,340	-5,811	-7,007	-3,879
22	Tripura	-29	-28	-30	-42	-33	-38
23	Utter Pradesh	-1,795	-807	-5,191	-7,730	-4,282	0
24	West Bengal	-542	-618	-2,444	-1,347	-1,289	-872
	Total	-5,022	-12,685	-18,769	-29,141	-18,540	-10,489

Source : Databank on SLPEs, Institute of Public Enterprise, Hyderbad.

Annexure-4

Internal Resource Generation By SLPEs During 1980-81 to 1986-87

	State	*80-81*	*81-82*	*82-83*	*83-84*	*84-85*	*85-86*	*86-87*
	Category A							
1	Retained Earnings	5,551	5,844	7,404	6,720	8,317	2,707	2938.8
2	Depreciation & DRE	1,297	1,364	1,846	2,662	2,502	9,007	9724.9
3	Gross Internal Resources	6,849	7,208	9,249	9,382	10,819	11,714	12663.7
	Category -B							
4	Retained Earnings	-6,784	-7,146	-823	-8,646	-10,416	-9,710	-11867.2
5	Depreciation & DRE	8,987	8,146	9,285	11,286	11,286	10,732	16097.6
6	Gross Internal Resources	2,203	1,000	1,002	1,499	870	1,022	4230.4
	Category - C							
7	Retained Earnings	-27,779	-32,553	-40,553	-43,154	-36,336	-35,941	-40529
8	Depreciation & DRE	6,753	7,188	9,590	10,104	15,699	18,643	27965.1
9	Gross Internal Resources	-21,026	-25,365	-30,963	-33,050	-20,637	-17,297	-12563.8
	Category A	6,849	7,208	9,249	9,382	10,819	11,714	12663.7
	Category B	2,203	1,000	1,002	1,499	870	1,022	4230.4
	Category C	-21,026	-25,365	-30,963	-33,050	-20,637	-17,297	-12563.8
	Total (A+B+C)	-11,975	-17,157	-20,712	-22,169	-8,948	-4,561	4330.4

Source : Databank on SLPEs, Institute of Public Enterprise, Hyderbad.

Annexure -5

Accumulated loss to Paid-up Capital in SLPEs

	State	81-82	82-83	83-84	84-85	85-86	86-87
1	Andhra Pradesh	30	32	33	36	40	42
2	Arunachal Pradesh	59	51	58	63	68	69
3	Assam	28	34	38	42	44	47
4	Bihar	31	40	47	54	62	68
5	Goa	3	3	3	3	4	4
6	Gujarat	18	19	20	22	28	30
7	Haryana	32	38	41	48	52	66
8	Himachal Pradesh	14	21	35	41	56	59
9	Jammu & Kishmir	10	12	18	20	21	24
10	Karnataka	16	14	32	39	52	70
11	Kerala	17	19	21	23	30	34
12	Madhya Pradesh	18	18	20	22	23	25
13	Maharashtra	35	36	38	42	43	-
14	Manipur	1	1	1	2	2	2

(Contd...)

15	Meghalaya	20	21	22	25	28	29
16	Misoram	1	1	1	1	1	1
17	Nagaland	35	35	38	40	424	345
18	Orissa	35	38	42	46	49	51
19	Punjab	-	-	-	-	-	-
20	Rajasthan	78	99	151	169	192	231
21	Tamil Nadu	47	42	58	62	51	68
22	Tripura	5	5	6	8	9	11
23	West Bengal	37	41	44	53	53	-

Source : Databank on SLPEs, Institute of Public Enterprise, Hyderbad.

Annexure - 6

Top Ten Enterprises in Terms of Profit (During the year 1986-87

Rs in Lakh

Sl.No.	*Name of the Entrprise*	*Profit*
1	The Singareni Colleries Co. Ltd.	4380.39
2	Leather Industries Development Corp. Ltd.	799.23
3	Travancore Tatium Products Ltd.	566.87
4	Karnataka State Financial Corp.	440.18
5	Kerala Civil Supplies Corp.	438
6	Gujarat Mineral Development Corp.	403.56
7	State Indu. & Investment Corp. of Maharashtra Ltd.	357.22
8	New Government Electricity Factory	291.94
9	Tamil Industrial Investment Corp.	281.52
10	Hyderabad Allwyn	281.36

Source : Databank on SLPEs, Institute of Public Enterprise, Hyderbad.

Annexure - 7

Top Ten Enterprise in terms of Accumulated Losses (during the year 1986)

Rs in Lakh

Sl.No.	*Name of the Entrprise*	*Profit*
1	Tamil Nadu Civil Supplies	17914.43
2	Visvaraya Iron and Steel Ltd.	13972.99
3	UP State Sugar Corpn.	12233.36
4	Durgapur Project Ltd.	6771.18
5	UP State Cement Corp.	5681.49
6	Kerala Minerals and Metals Ltd.	4473.97
7	Durgapur Chemicals Ltd.	4265.21
8	Tamil Nadu News Prints and Papers Ltd.	4025.05
9	Kalyani Spinning Mills	3770.83
10	Transfors and Electricals Ltd.	3547.01

Source : Databank on SLPEs, Institute of Public Enterprise, Hyderbad.

Annexure - 8

Distribution of SLPEs in Different Sectors

Sl.No.	State	Manufacturing	Trading	Finance	Promotional	Welfare	Total
1	Andhra Pradesh	8	5	2	17	4	36
2	Arunachal Pradesh	-	1	1	1	-	3
3	Assam	19	2	2	14	6	43
4	Bihar	9	12	4	16	6	47
5	Goa	4	-	1	2	-	7
6	Gujarat	17	8	5	16	2	48
7	Haryana	5	6	2	6	3	22
8	Himachal Pradesh	6	5	1	5	-	17
9	Jammu & Kishmir	7	2	2	5	-	16
10	Karnataka	2	11	12	19	5	58
11	Kerala	47	16	4	13	10	90
12	Madhya Pradesh	8	3	2	8	11	32
13	Maharashtra	16	4	4	15	12	51

(Contd...)

14	Manipur	2	1	1	2	2	8
15	Meghalaya	4	1	1	3	-	9
16	Misoram	-	-	1	1	1	3
17	Nagaland	1	2	1	-	1	5
18	Orissa	6	9	2	14	2	33
19	Punjab	1	6	2	11	4	25
20	Rajasthan	15	4	3	10	4	36
21	Tamil Nadu	15	5	4	17	3	44
22	Tripura	1	4	1	-	1	7
23	Utter Pradesh	14	7	3	21	16	61
24	West Bengal	24	7	2	20	-	53

Source : Databank on SLPEs, Institute of Public Enterprise, Hyderbad.

Annexure - 9

Capital Investment in Manufacturing SLPEs

Rs in Crores

Sl.No.	State	81-82	82-83	83-84	84-85	85-86	86-87
1	Andhra Pradesh	27,943.00	36,419.00	49,260.00	51,446.00	50,203.00	53,202.00
2	Assam	3964	4958	5719	7963	9004	10890
3	Bihar	6,197.00	9,178.00	11,519.00	13,139.00	17,839.00	21,544.00
4	Goa	165.00	170.00	180.00	220.00	290.00	330.00
5	Gujarat	4200	5910	7503	8713	10585	10736
6	Haryana	750.00	880.00	910.00	940.00	980.00	1,068.00
7	Himachal Pradesh	829	938	981	1008	1,140.00	1,271.00
8	Jammu & Kishmir	2,929.00	3,381.00	4,581.00	5,808.00	6,453.00	7,549.00
9	Karnataka	44890	47748	50440	52271	54118	60529
10	Kerala	27,016.00	33,430.00	39,789.00	42,447.00	44,698.00	46,605.00
11	Madhya Pradesh	1,840.00	1,920.00	2,140.00	2,860.00	3,240.00	3,876.00
12	Maharashtra	5840	6077	6251	7952	6795	7851
13	Manipur	394.00	410.00	456.00	520.00	580.00	627.00

(Contd...)

14	Meghalaya	920	970	1040	1210	1485	1726
15	Nagaland	294	348	360	384	420	496
16	Orissa	7944	9270	10717	12853	14251	15244
17	Punjab	74	80	84	91	98	113
18	Rajasthan	3,100.00	3,963.00	4,630.00	4,977.00	5,676.00	5,743.00
19	Tamil Nadu	15662	16023	36755	40014	41643	45514
20	Tripura	910.00	980.00	1,060.00	1,140.00	1,310.00	1,515.00
21	Utter Pradesh	21,505.00	28,051.00	34,820.00	39,946.00	45,802.00	49,575.00
22	West Bengal	17840	24182	27208	30202	32856	37654
	Total	195,206.00	235,286.00	296,403.00	326,104.00	349,466.00	383,658.00

Source : Databank on SLPEs, Institute of Public Enterprise, Hyderbad.

Annexure - 10

Rate of Return in Manufacturing SLPEs

Sl.No.	State	81-82	82-83	83-84	84-85	85-86	86-87
1	Andhra Pradesh	10.02	0.72	-3.12	-1.78	17.79	15.29
2	Assam	NA	NA	NA	NA	0	0
3	Bihar	-11.92	-2.54	-2.54	-2.54	-2.54	-2.54
4	Goa	5.89	7.85	10.75	35.07	49.11	49.11
5	Gujarat	-8.3	-2.23	-1.41	-1.2	-3.62	-3.62
6	Haryana	NA	NA	NA	0.00	0.00	0.00
7	Himachal Pradesh	-0.32	-0.32	0.47	0.38	1.52	1.52
8	Jammu & Kishmir	NA	NA	0.45	16.56	4.70	4.70
9	Karnataka	4.65	-3.96	-2.59	-0.28	0.78	2.49
10	Kerala	3.71	0.16	0.22	-3.03	-0.35	0.28
11	Madhya Pradesh	NA	5.68	5.41	5.41	5.41	5.41
12	Maharashtra	4.04	3.92	-0.32	0.12	0.94	-0.05
13	Manipur	NA	NA	NA	0.00	0.00	0.00
14	Meghalaya	NA	NA	NA	0	0	0

(Contd...)

15	Nagaland	-20.61	-17.54	-3.81	0	0	0
16	Orissa	-2.85	5.23	3.53	3.93	5.68	3.71
17	Punjab	0.72	-3.39	-3.98	-1.26	0	0
18	Rajasthan	1.32	12.26	25.31	0.35	-3.48	-3.48
19	Tamil Nadu	5.02	-2.72	1.46	0.06	4.54	2.25
20	Tripura	NA	NA	NA	0.00	5.69	5.69
21	Utter Pradesh	0.24	4.35	-3.61	-3.13	0.70	1.83
22	West Bengal	-1.07	0.92	-5.62	-1.14	-0.17	-0.02
23	Meghalaya	-1.76	-0.55	-0.84	-0.84	-0.84	-0.84
		-0.48782608	0.34086956	0.859130435	2.029565217	3.73304348	3.5534783

Source : Databank on SLPEs, Institute of Public Enterprise, Hyderbad.

Annexure - 11

State-wise Distribution of Manufacturing SLPEs

Sl.No.	*State*	*Total No. of SLPEs*	*A*	*B*	*C*	*D*	*E*	*F*	*G*
1	Andhra Pradesh	8	4	-	1	2	-	1	-
2	Arunachal Pradesh	-	-	-	-	-	-	-	-
3	Assam	49	6	4	4	2	1	2	-
4	Bihar	9	1	2	1	1	2	1	1
5	Goa	4	2	2	-	-	-	-	-
6	Gujarat	17	4	3	1	1	-	-	1
7	Haryana	5	2	2	-	1	-	-	-
8	Himachal Pradesh	6	1	2	-	1	-	-	-
9	Jammu & Kishmir	7	1	-	-	1	-	-	1
10	Karnataka	21	6	1	2	2	2	1	-
11	Kerala	47	7	10	3	2	3	1	1
12	Madhya Pradesh	8	1	-	1	2	-	-	-
13	Maharashtra	16	1	-	6	1	1	-	-
14	Manipur	2		1	-	-		1	-

(Contd...)

15	Meghalaya	4		-	-	1		-	1
16	Misoram	-		-	-	-		-	-
17	Nagaland	1		-	-	-		1	-
18	Orissa	6		2	2	1		-	-
19	Punjab	1		-	-	-		-	-
20	Rajasthan	15	2	1	-	2		1	-
21	Tamil Nadu	15	3	1	2	1		2	1
22	Tripura	1	-	-	-	-		-	-
23	Uttar Pradesh	14	-	4	4	1	1	3	1
24	West Bengal	24	8	4	3	1	2	1	-
	Total	250	49	39	30	23	12	15	7

Source : Databank on SLPEs, Institute of Public Enterprise, Hyderbad.
A-Engineering E- Drugs & Chemicals
B- Electronics F- Sugar C-Textiles G - Cements D Mining H- Others.

Annexure 12

Capital Investment in Trading and Services SLPEs

SL No	State	81-82	82-83	83-84	84-85	85-86	86-87
1	Andhra Pradesh	3,344.00	4,237.00	4,693.00	5,403.00	6,457.00	7,840.00
2	Arunachal Pradesh	6	7	7	8	8	10
3	Assam	1,473.00	1,721.00	2,077.00	2,541.00	3,160.00	4,690.00
4	Bihar	1,632.00	3,725.00	4,576.00	6,270.00	11,038.00	13,435.00
5	Gujarat	561	1158	1455	2061	2658	3763
6	Haryana	11,308.00	12,144.00	12,840.00	13,113.00	14,830.00	18,286.00
7	Himachal Pradesh	1862	2091	2703	3100	3,253.00	3,711.00
8	Jammu & Kashmir	650.00	790.00	834.00	1,109.00	1,615.00	2,179.00
9	Karnataka	6867	8014	8639	9386	10800	11894
10	Kerala	6,405.00	6,618.00	7,000.00	8,969.00	9,282.00	10,807.00
11	Madhya Pradesh	820.00	980.00	1,140.00	1,320.00	1,450.00	1,664.00
12	Maharashtra	820	860	980	1140	1302	1483
13	Manipur	85.00	91.00	98.00	104.00	110.00	122.00
14	Meghalaya	15	16	16	17	21	28
15	Orissa	2092	2381	2810	3050	325	3756
16	Punjab	30460	33790	39175	42140	48650	53954
17	Rajasthan	1715	1765	1782	1885	2990	3203
18	Tamil Nadu	2,557.00	2,827.00	3,497.00	3,932.00	4,109.00	4,429.00
19	Uttar Pradesh	4947	6917	7031	8020	9043	13031
20	West Bengal	110.00	143.00	274.00	327.00	419.00	490.00
	Total	77,729.00	90,275.00	101,627.00	113,895.00	131,520.00	158,775.00

Source : Databank on SLPEs, Institute of Public Enterprise, Hyderbad.

* Data pertaining to years 1984-85 have been repeated for the years 1985-86 and 1986-87.

Annexure 13

Rate of Return in Trading and Marketing SLPEs

SL No	State	81-82	82-83	83-84	84-85	85-86	86-87
1	Andhra Pradesh	4.46	-2.03	2.50	4.48	10.60	11.85
2	Assam	NA	NA	NA	NA	NA	NA
3	Bihar	-0.33	-0.18	-0.60	-0.52	-0.52	-0.50
4	Goa	0.98	1.32	0.55	0.99	0.86	0.86
5	Gujarat	84.71	89.34	16.21	35.94	34.68	34.68
6	Haryana	5.36	-1.90	3.59	12.01	12.11	12.11
7	Himachal Pradesh	4.18	5.93	8.86	7.55	7.55	7.55
8	Jammu & Kashmir	NA	NA	1.27	2.15	2.15	2.15
9	Karnataka	3.96	4.28	4.9	4.54	5.71	6.35
10	Kerala	2.47	-0.82	3.58	19.46	5.92	12.41
11	Madhya Pradesh	NA	2.95	1.27	2.24	2.24	2.24
12	Maharashtra	-7.82	-5.02	-3.14	-12.83	-2.17	-2.78
13	Manipur	NA	NA	NA	NA	NA	NA
14	Mizoram	NA	NA	NA	NA	NA	NA

(Contd...)

15	Nagaland	NA	NA	NA	NA	NA	NA
16	Orissa	9.94	9.94	28.2	16.76	35.38	15.63
17	Punjab	0.53	0.65	-1.88	-3.86	NA	NA
18	Rajasthan	2.12	-5.44	-4.00	7.57	14.41	14.41
19	Tamil Nadu	-3.02	-104.15	-74.36	-65.57	-25.36	7.84
20	Tripura	NA	NA	NA	NA	NA	NA
21	Uttar Pradesh	11.38	9.35	4.52	9.92	1.66	16.25
22	West Bengal	0.90	5.58	-2.64	-1.90	3.90	3.90
23	Meghalaya	40.83	35.68	47.3	47.3	47.3	47.3
	Average	6.98	1.99	1.61	3.75	7.42	8.32

Source : Databank on SLPEs, Institute of Public Enterprise, Hyderbad.

NA -Not Available

Annexure - 14

Capital Investment in Financial SLPEs

in crores

SL No	*State*	*81-82*	*82-83*	*83-84*	*84-85*	*85-86*	*86-87*
1	Andhra Pradesh	18,224.00	21,688.00	26,656.00	30,869.00	38,281.00	43,701.00
2	Arunachal Pradesh	220	231	262	284	310	363
3	Assam	3,034.00	4,168.00	4,177.00	5,159.00	5,972.00	6,975.00
4	Bihar	1,821.00	2,048.00	4,665.00	10,085.00	12,060.00	15,805.00
5	Goa	1990	2260	2610	2840	3200	3589
6	Gujarat	23,151.00	27,069.00	29,740.00	33,060.00	38,517.00	45,407.00
7	Haryana	6100	6800	7714	9860	10,530.00	11,394.00
8	Himachal Pradesh	2,450.00	2,800.00	3,650.00	3,900.00	4,200.00	4,600.00
9	Jammu & Kashmir	4543	5334	6354	7148	8148	9250
10	Karnataka	12,468.00	15,717.00	19,626.00	23,619.00	30,037.00	37,334.00
11	Kerala	9,946.00	11,347.00	12,460.00	14,056.00	15,260.00	16,734.00
13	Maharashtra	40232	44078	50083	63574	76701	83197
14	Manipur	75.00	83.00	92.00	102.00	108.00	110.00

(Contd...)

15	Meghalaya	840	950	980	1080	1140	1278
16	Mizoram	510	580	625	740	820	943
17	Nagaland	540	608	680	714	792	847
18	Orissa	6648	9115	14898	16223	18956	20337
19	Punjab	8,090.00	9,150.00	9,840.00	10,850.00	12,140.00	13,820.00
20	Rajasthan	15290	20404	25033	29191	33185	37637
21	Tamil Nadu	30,017.00	33,451.00	36,937.00	40,628.00	45,373.00	48,028.00
22	Tripura	120.00	148.00	148.00	153.00	158.00	161.00
23	Uttar Pradesh	2,199.00	29,568.00	29,568.00	39,947.00	50,001.00	61,628.00
24	West Bengal	9468	13223	13223	15599	17980	18750
	Total	197976	260820	300021	359681	423869	481888

Source : Databank on SLPEs, Institute of Public Enterprise, Hyderbad.

Annexure 15

Rate of Return in Financial SLPEs

SL No	*State*	*81-82*	*82-83*	*83-84*	*84-85*	*85-86*	*86-87*
1	Andhra Pradesh	5.49	6.47	6.85	7.25	6.78	5.15
2	Assam	NA	NA	NA	NA	NA	NA
3	Bihar	NA	NA	NA	NA	NA	NA
4	Goa	0.00	0.00	5.10	5.64	5.34	5.34
5	Gujarat	4.84	6.22	6.93	6.94	7.55	7.55
6	Haryana	0.00	2.56	2.42	4.12	4.12	4.12
7	Himachal Pradesh	0	0	0	0	0.00	0.00
8	Jammu & Kashmir	4.54	4.92	4.94	4.95	4.95	4.95
9	Karnataka	2.48	2.36	0.95	0.83	2.43	3.14
10	Kerala	5.11	3.96	5.24	5.60	5.94	6.65
11	Madhya Pradesh	NA	NA	NA	NA	NA	NA
12	Maharashtra	4.53	3.48	3.7	9.38	8.75	9.85
13	Manipur	NA	NA	NA	NA	NA	NA
14	Mizoram	4.86	4.83	4.86	2.68	2.69	2.69

(Contd...)

15	Nagaland	NA	NA	2.63	2.18	NA	NA
16	Orissa	5.24	6.15	1.82	4.53	3.88	0.97
17	Punjab	7.89	4.21	4.56	2.7	NA	NA
18	Rajasthan	3.21	3.94	0.78	-0.07	-0.16	-0.16
19	Tamil Nadu	6.08	6.4	6.13	5.41	4.41	4.93
20	Tripura	NA	NA	3.06	3.06	3.06	3.06
21	Uttar Pradesh	11.29	5.86	5.90	5.27	5.87	6.46
22	West Bengal	5.31	5.58	6.54	6.14	7.68	7.68
23	Meghalaya	NA	NA	NA	NA	NA	NA
	Average	2.96	2.65	2.94	3.29	3.1	3.13

Source : Databank on SLPEs, Institute of Public Enterprise, Hyderbad.
NA -Not Available

Annexure 16

Capital Investment in Promotional SLPEs

in crores

SL No	State	81-82	82-83	83-84	84-85	85-86	86-87
1	Andhra Pradesh	10,841.00	12,080.00	13,739.00	16,373.00	17,712.00	26,341.00
2	Arunachal Pradesh	192	210	244	260	290	332
3	Assam	1,511.00	1,914.00	2,529.00	2,619.00	3,425.00	4,079.00
4	Bihar	4,641.00	15,811.00	16,130.00	18,019.00	21,256.00	22,106.00
5	Goa	77	72	90	95	104	115
6	Gujarat	4,443.00	5,276.00	6,327.00	7,739.00	8,642.00	11,242.00
7	Haryana	2280	2645	3140	3650	3,800.00	4,660.00
8	Himachal Pradesh	1,703.00	1,946.00	2,347.00	2,657.00	2,948.00	3,403.00
9	Jammu & Kashmir	1023	1023	1031	1333	1391	1416
10	Karnataka	5,599.00	6,999.00	7,446.00	8,507.00	10,360.00	11,865.00
11	Kerala	4,630.00	5,033.00	6,146.00	7,635.00	11,682.00	12,979.00
12	Madhya Pradesh	3220	3940	4340	4890	5150	5339
13	Maharashtra	9,572.00	10,786.00	11,879.00	12,518.00	14,610.00	18,826.00

(Contd...)

14	Manipur	195	222	248	280	294	332
15	Nagaland	114	150	163	172	184	212
16	Orissa	580	665	710	760	880	974
17	Punjab	9378	10602	11198	13083	15131	15794
18	Rajasthan	3,319.00	3,430.00	3,780.00	3,960.00	4,290.00	4,922.00
19	Tamil Nadu	8731	8987	9662	10406	11380	12810
20	Tripura	3,917.00	3,451.00	3,957.00	4,628.00	5,373.00	6,260.00
21	Uttar Pradesh	515.00	590.00	620.00	680.00	765.00	885.00
22	West Bengal	5,501.00	7,663.00	10,565.00	12,171.00	13,421.00	15,620.00
23	Meghalaya	5835	9307	11241	12664	13306	15488
	Total	87817	112802	127532	145099	166394	196000

Source : Databank on SLPEs, Institute of Public Enterprise, Hyderbad.

Annexure 17

Rate of Return in Promotional SLPEs

SL No	State	81-82	82-83	83-84	84-85	85-86	86-87
1	Andhra Pradesh	1.66	3.3	3.58	2.81	4.88	5.65
2	Assam	NA	NA	NA	NA	NA	NA
3	Bihar	-0.21	1.16	-2.21	0.72	-0.10	-0.10
4	Goa	NA	NA	NA	NA	NA	NA
5	Gujarat	5.94	10.28	22.78	13.18	7.84	7.84
6	Haryana	5.41	-0.46	3.2	3.56	3.27	3.27
7	Himachal Pradesh	5.14	4.57	4.55	4.36	4.21	4.21
8	Jammu & Kashmir	NA	NA	-2.98	-7.97	-1.74	-1.74
9	Karnataka	1.33	3.03	4.47	5.04	4.37	4.89
10	Kerala	2.30	1.24	-1.64	-1.29	-1.27	-0.51
11	Madhya Pradesh	NA	-0.53	3.37	4.38	2.4	2.4
12	Maharashtra	3.24	2.11	-1.98	-1.01	0.71	0.57
13	Manipur	-2.67	-3.2	-3.2	-2.32	-2.32	-2.32
14	Mizoram	NA	NA	NA	NA	NA	NA

(Contd...)

15	Nagaland	NA	NA	NA	NA	NA	NA
16	Orissa	-0.69	-3	-4	-2.74	-2.85	-3.06
17	Punjab	-6.71	-4.84	-6.10	-5.76	NA	NA
18	Rajasthan	0.56	0.69	-3.2	-4.36	-2.04	-2.04
19	Tamil Nadu	2.31	2.63	6.18	5.87	6.02	8.21
20	Tripura	1.07	1.07	1.07	1.07	1.07	1.07
21	Uttar Pradesh	0.96	1.54	0.64	0.15	0.25	0.59
22	West Bengal	-3.78	-3.07	0.42	0.90	-1.26	-1.26
23	Meghalaya	-6.22	-9.58	-4.11	-3.85	-3.83	-3.85
	Average	0.33	0.22	0.33	0.51	0.89	1.43

Source : Databank on SLPEs, Institute of Public Enterprise, Hyderbad.
NA -Not Available.

Annexure 18

Capital Investment in Welfare SLPEs

in crores

Sl.No.	State	81-82	82-83	83-84	84-85	85-86	86-87
1	Andhra Pradesh	2,227.00	2,592.00	3,835.00	3,665.00	4,255.00	5,370.00
2	Assam	126	199	257	303	404	446
3	Bihar	1,985.00	2,195.00	3,441.00	4,995.00	5,040.00	4,721.00
4	Gujarat	1,475.00	1,533.00	1,668.00	1,810.00	1,931.00	2,392.00
5	Haryana	860	910	991	1080	1240	1615
6	Karnataka	721.00	1,021.00	1,215.00	1,411.00	1,850.00	2,135.00
7	Kerala	245	334	386	450	650.00	731.00
8	Madhya Pradesh	890.00	820.00	980.00	4,060.00	1,240.00	4,638.00
9	Maharashtra	4302	6517	7393	6805	7849	8493
10	Manipur	31.00	38.00	47.00	52.00	58.00	63.00
11	Orissa	0.00	0.00	185.00	235.00	237.00	319.00
12	Punjab	1230	1485	1675	1830	2140	2761
13	Rajasthan	911.00	960.00	1,068.00	1,154.00	1,274.00	1,308.00
14	Tamil Nadu	1008	980	1186	1235	1675	1363
15	Uttar Pradesh	6205	8592	9566	11290	12507	13619
	Total	22216	28176	33893	40375	42350	49974

Source: Databank on SLPEs, Institute of Public Enterprise, Hyderbad.

Annexure 19

Rate of Return in Welfare SLPEs

Sl. No.	State	1981-1982	1982-1983	1983-1984	1984-1985	1985-1986	1986-1987
1	Andhra Pradesh	3.06	0.63	2.34	1.37	1.27	1.16
2	Assam	NA	NA	NA	NA	NA	NA
3	Bihar	-2.06	14.50	-2.38	-1.91	-1.91	-1.91
4	Goa	NA	NA	NA	NA	NA	NA
5	Gujarat	2.56	2.21	4.41	3.43	8.11	8.11
6	Haryana	-6.79	-5.59	4.75	4.63	4.63	4.63
7	Himachal Pradesh	NA	NA	NA	NA	NA	NA
8	Jammu & Kashmir	NA	NA	NA	NA	NA	NA
9	Karnataka	7.77	14.33	6.9	6.35	10.34	10.6
10	Kerala	-23.29	-16.56	6.77	4.11	3.48	3.08
11	Madhya Pradesh	NA	-6.88	-4.46	-3.19	-3.19	-3.19
12	Maharashtra	1.64	1.16	0.89	3.72	4.38	5.56
13	Manipur	-9.04	-4.35	-58.00	-28.56	-69.89	-69.89
14	Mizoram	NA	NA	NA	NA	NA	NA

(Contd...)

15	Nagaland	NA	NA	NA	NA	NA	NA
16	Orissa	NA	NA	-4.62	-4.28	-3.49	-1.84
17	Punjab	1.42	-0.24	0.09	-0.17	NA	NA
18	Rajasthan	NA	NA	NA	NA	NA	NA
19	Tamil Nadu	NA	NA	-6.15	6.21	2.5	7.19
20	Tripura	NA	NA	NA	NA	NA	NA
21	Uttar Pradesh	0.20	3.60	-1.13	-9.58	-5.08	-4.51
22	West Bengal	8.79	-24.14	-15.35	-7.44	-7.82	-7.82
	Average	2.42	-0.97	-3.00	-1.15	-2.58	-2.22

Source : Databank on SLPEs, Institute of Public Enterprise, Hyderbad.
NA -Not Available

9

Non- Privatisation Reforms in State Level Public Enterprises (SLPEs)*

Introduction

The objectives and composition of SLPEs are different form that of Central Public Enterprises (CPEs) in India. While 75 per cent of central enterprises come under the manufacturing and service sector only about 30 per cent of SLPEs fall under this category.

SECTION - I

BOARD LEVEL REFORMS

Corporatisation

Though SLPEs have been formed as joint stock companies, they merely remain in legal form, whereas they still operate as the extended arm of the state government. Over 90 per cent of SLPEs continue to be headed by civil servants as CEOs and

* Professor & Chairman, Corporate and General Management Division, Institute of Public Enterprise, O.U.Campus, Hyderabad-500 007

public figures as chairmen. These enterprises follow the departmental policies, procedures and culture; continuity of the top management is very limited. While at even junior levels persons are drawn on deputation from state government. A study conducted in the Institute reveals that 40 per cent of the SLPEs are awfully in arrears in finalisation of their annual accounts. There are enterprises, which have not compiled their annual accounts for the past 8 to 10 years. The story is not much different in respect of budget formulation and its review. The basic principles of ensuring corporate autonomy of management through the installation of budgetary control, management information system and cost and efficiency standards are non-existent in most cases.

Tenure of Chief Executive of SLPEs

As stated earlier most SLPEs depend on civil servants to man the top management positions. This is the case even after 2 decades of the formation of SLPEs in India. It has not been possible to professionalise the top management.

There is strong argument that SLPEs by virtue of their dominant public purpose and close interaction on matters of policy with state government, should fill-up their top management positions through civil servants who cannot be suitably accommodated in government or politicians who are unsuccessful in elections or who cannot be accommodated in the cabinet. While it may genuinely require to have public figures manning top positions in the SLPEs in order to give expression to peoples aspirations and needs, their position, role and activities in the management of there enterprises is a matter for serious discussions. If SLPEs are to be truly corporatised reforms are needed in the composition of the board and its personnel. A study of the tenure and profile of SLPE chief executives from a sample of 35 enterprises covering the various sectors over a span of almost 2 decades, provide interesting insight into their corporate management.

Table 9.1 Per cent distribution of Tenure of Chief Executives of SLPEs.

Sl.No	*CEs Tenure Range (in months)*	*Sample Base*	*Per cent Distribution*	*Cumulative Per cent*
1	1	17	12.14	12.14
2	1-3	21	15.00	27.14
3	3-6	21	15.00	42.14
4	6-9	9	6.42	48.56
5	9-12	10	7.14	55.70
6	12-18	23	16.43	72.63
7	18-24	15	10.71	82.84
8	24-30	4	2.86	85.70
9	30-36	4	2.86	88.56
10	36-60	10	7.14	95.70
11	Over 5 years	6	4.30	100.00
	Total	140	100.00	

Table 9.1 shows that over 27 per cent of chief executives have ridiculously short and less than 3 months tenure. More that 56 per cent stay with the SLPEs for less than a year. The average tenure comes to 15 months. This is a dismal picture when compared to the central enterprises, or the recommendations by expert committees such as Krishna Menon Committee, Kapoor Committee,, Arjun Sengupta Committee. This is the most important area to be studied by all state governments and SLPEs and urgent reforms are called to ensure a reasonable tenure of 2 to 3 years to the CEOs in the SLPEs.

An analysis of the profile of the persons posted as CEOs of the SLPEs confirm the earlier hypothesis that they are mostly drawn form IAS (75 per cent). The technical and professional managers headings SLPEs are only about 13 per cent. Even among these technical persons some are on deputation from PWD and irrigation departments in the state governments. Thus 90 per cent of the chief executives heading the SLPEs are deputationists. A profile of CEOs posted to the SLPEs is shown below:

Table 9.2 Profile of the Chief Executives

SL.No	*Background*	*Per cent*	*No. of Appointments*	*No. of postings with Tenure over 3 years*	*Tenure exceeding 5 years*
1	IAS	74.28	104	10	1
2	IPS/IFS	9.28	13	1	-
3	State Cadre Officers	3.57	5	-	-
4	Technical/ Professional Managers	12.85	18	5	5
		100.00	140	16	6

It is not easy to seek reasons for the frequent changes in the incumbanacy of the CEO of the SLPEs. It is often reported that all changes were made in "Public interest". Does it means that the interest of the SLPEs is not in "Public good" ?

Board Level Reforms

All the boards of the SLPEs with very few exceptions are part time boards. In the case of SLPEs it is the state government, which formulate and determine operational strategies. The size of boards of the SLPEs are large ranging from 5 to 15 persons with an average being about 11. The following takes analyses and examines the size and composition of the board of SLPEs on a sample basis.

It is observed that in the case of promotional and service enterprises more than 53 per cent of board members belong to the public figures category and another 34 per cent turned out to be the nominees of the state governments. For all the boards the composition reveals that 45 per cent are public figures, 32 per cent are ex-officio members, 10 per cent are CEOs and only

Table 9.3 Composition of the Boards

Sl.No	*Nature of enterprise*	*No. of enterprises*	*Size Min*	*Range Max*	*Public figures*	*Ex-officio*	*Chief executive*	*Experts professional nominees*	*Insiders*
1	Promotional and Service (not for profit alone type)	15	9	15	53%	34%	9%	4%	-
2	Manufacturing Trading (Profit oriented)	10	5	10	25%	28%	12%	25%	10%
	All	25	5	15	45% Av=11	32%	10%	10%	3%

about 10 per cent experts and professionals. The insiders are almost negligible constituting 3 percent of the strength of the board of SLPEs broadly all the SLPEs taken together. It can safely be argued that more than 55 per cent of members of the board of the SLPEs are non-professionals and there is hardly any representation form within the enterprise. A few exceptions are in the case of SEBs.

As a first stage of reforms for SLPEs, Corporatisation with an increased professionalisation of boards is a pre-requisite. However, it has already been argued that SLPEs boards are sub- policy and more operational in character; and therefore there is strong justification to induct corporate managers into the board.

One good guideline could be that board, should have 1/3rd representation form each of the major stakeholders namely public figures, government officials and internal managers. This way the ground could be set to establish continuity in management at the top level and also to give effect to the long term policies of the board, even if the chief executives are changed in between.

Another possible reform is to have a tow-tier board. This will amount to having at the apex level, a policy board and at the lower level an executive committee. The policy board could comprise exclusively part-time members while the executive boards would consist of the Chairman, MD, two or there internal director. An alternative to this is to have an entirely professional board consisting of Chairman and MD and functional director. In this scheme of the things chairman represent the public while the MDs role is that of a nominee of the government and the rest of the board could be drawn from internal managers and workers. For wider consultation and interaction each enterprise could have a standing consultative committee of public figures and connected institutions.

Worker participation

This has by and large remained a concept and remains yet

to be put into practice. Large enterprises like SEBs and RTCs where trade union function has fairly stabilized, workers participation at board level remains a much awaited refrom.

SECTION II

ORGANISATION RESTRUCTURING

Merger

Several SLPEs are very small in size. It is more true specifically in the cases of small manufacturing, trading and welfare corporations. For example separate corporations exist in all state for the welfare of the SCs /STs, BCs, Women and Tribal. Though their target groups are different, their operational strategy, procedures and geographic area are more or less same. All such SLPEs face the common problems of shortage of staff, dearth of adequate funds and uncongenial interface with the state governments. Similar is the case with large number of manufacturing units, mostly taken over sick units having individual manufacturing and marketing facilities and uneconomic size of operations. In AP SLPEs like Krishi Engines, Republic Forge, Hyderabad Allwyn, AP Scooters, AP Heavy Engg come under this category. Similarly one can suggest merger as a good approach to overcome the problems of uneconomic scale. The third strong candidate for establishing common organisation linkages is the SLPEs operating in the housing sector. The state housing development corporation, weaker sections housing societies, police housing corporation need to be clubbed together.

Therefore, merger of related corporations cited above is considered to be in the direction of inducing operational efficiency. The major advantages that could be obtained from such reforms are as follows.

Achieving optimal size: The fragmented organisation all working towards the same purpose can be grouped together to gain considerable size and strength. The overheads can also be considerably reduced; planning and control can be made more professional.

By amalgamation of related SLPEs, operating synergy can be improved. This would be akin to a well developed related company.

Such amalgamation would provide efficient forward and backward linkages, better marketing, forecasting and planning facilities besides scope for R & D in the case of manufacturing enterprises.

It is well known that a large enterprise would be able to enhance its credibality with financial institution and increase its borrowing capacity. Most of SLPEs are primarily set up to mobilise institutional funds and therefore, an economical size is important consideration.

In the case of manufacturing and trading enterprises, merger could help tax saving especially a high profit making being merged with sick one.

As against those arguments, the strong opposition for such merger has come form the plea the;

a. By merger exclusive attention on a particular group may be lost and
b. Though un spelt, it would reduce opportunities at top level for civil servants and politicians who now head such corporations.

Common Boards / Holdings Cos

If outright mergers as discussed above are not possible then establishing common Boards, sector wise for welfare, promotion corporations can be thought of. In case of holding companies. This would reduce the number of such companies, allow top management more time for planning and provide greater attention to market development and R&D. Having common boards would also lead to greater professionalisation of corporate management.

Internal Restructuring

The SLPEs, being an off-shoot of government suffer all the hierarchical weaknesses of the government organisation. Normally, one notices 5-6 levels in the organisations structure of the SLPEs which is not conducive to quick decision making. What is needed in most of SLPEs in the promotional, development and welfare sectors is to have a three tier organisation to take care of viz i. Case preparation ii. Supervision and iii. Decision making, therefore restructuring the internal organisation to aid quick decision making is an essential reform.

SECTION -III

MANAGEMENT REFORMS

1. Memorandum of Understanding

A recent non -diverstiture option, following the recommendation of Sengupta Committee (1984) aimed towards improving PE performance, providing more autonomy to PE manager in the introduction of MOU. This has been selectively done in about 20 leading central enterprises. Though the impact of the introduction has not yet been systematically evaluated, it is generally felt that it has been able to generate a better understanding about the objectives and roles of PEs. It has also provided a framework for performance evaluation and given a greater operational autonomy to public enterprises. However, such managerial innovations have not been introduced in SLPEs in India. The need for MOU in SLPE is being discussed at various levels. However, it has yet to take an operational shape. Though the question of autonomy has remained unresolved in the SLPEs, it has never been a more important issue than the preparation by each such enterprises of statement of objectives, and goals and role to evaluate ultimately their performance. Therefore, an attempt to introduce MOU in the SLPEs to start with in large enterprises like SEB's , RTC's, could go a long way in bringing about a greater transparency in their performance.

2. Corporate Planning

The SLPEs are known to have multiple objectives and clear articulation of such objectives at enterprise level, both of short term and long term is an overdue exercise. Corporate Planning as a continuous managerial process is a totally neglected phenomenon in the SLPEs. The task of objectives setting analysis of new opportunities, threats and understanding special strengths and limitations should be taken on an ongoing basis by these enterprises. This can be then coupled with the MOU exercise, to give shape substance to Corporate Management. Once this is undertaken, the management of SLPEs become more transparent, future more visible and performance evaluation possible.

The SLPEs as a first step towards reform could undertake a one year Action Planning exercise, identifying their targets, social obligations and resources requirements, this was successfully done in AP for two years during 1984-85. But unfortunately it was given up later for unknown reasons.

3. Finalisation of Accounts and Financial Management

Almost 40 per cent of SLPEs are in arrears of their annual accounts. The submission of annual accounts is not only a legal requirement but their completion is important for evaluation of the performance. Whatever be the reasons for non-finalisation of accounts, greater emphasis should be attached to this to thwart.

10

Less Government or More Government ?

Twentieth century is remarkably different from earlier centuries in many respects- technologies, ideologies, economic growth, quality of life, information explosion violence - one could expand the list a much longer and have long debates on each item, but one fact will emerge undisputed that the role of Government in economy and the life of a citizen increased in an unprecedented manner during this century; in every country and under every ideological set up. After the World War II, in the erstwhile colonial countries as well as the newly independent countries, government expanded at a phenomenal rate -not only in size but also in terms of functions and responsibilities. India was no exception or rather would be one of the front runners in respect of the rate of expansion of Governments role. However, a serious thought is being given world over, as to whether the process needs to be halted, reversed or accelerated.

Planning Models

Development and Economic planning were two of the 20th century's greatest discoveries and were perhaps largely instrumental in increasing governmental intervention by providing a respectable and often moralistic justification. Countries generally followed one of the following models a. Communist Central Planning (USSR, Eastern Europe); b. Socialist 'mixed' economy planning (India and many more other developing countries) c. Indicative planning (France , Japan) and d. Market Economy (USA , EEC countries). There were some mixed models too. For example in countries like South Korea and Taiwan, governments regulated the economies but did not curb the private sector. Some countries followed a particular model (with modifications) and then changed course radically. For example, in UK and France, public sector was very prominent at one time but considerable privatisation and deregulation occurred subsequently. One more point must be made, non of these models were mutually exclusive. Even in the free market economies, governments assumed greater developmental responsibilities such as infrastructure development, social services or rehabilitation of sick industries etc. or regulatory functions. Communist and Socialist models called for a much higher degree of governmental action than the other models.

Another important factor (not unrelated) was the social services sector- health, education social security which was responsible for involving governments more actively. In this respect also, certain models can be discerned, roughly corresponding to the economic planning models:-

1. Communist model in which the state assumed full responsibility for providing all social services.
2. Residual model in which the individual family and the voluntary sector were primarily responsible for welfare and rehabilitative care or market instruments such as insurance and pension funds played their part.
3. Welfare mode, which essentially resembled the residual model but the State was a lot more active and egalitarian e.g. Scandinavian Countries.

As in economic planning in this sector also we find many examples of mixed models; a remarkable shift in the emphasis over a period in some of the countries and that the choice of a model usually determined the degree of governmental involvement.

Whichever model a country adopted and to whatever degree the bureaucracies expanded phenomenally everywhere. In UK, for instance, there were more employees on the government's payroll after the empire was disbanded that during the colonial period. The government 'spending' also increased substantially in every country and to raise resources, governments resorted increasingly to raising tax levels, deficit financing and running up debts.

Economic growth

To these board generalisations, which are more or less non-controversial one could add another (perhaps a debatable one) that whenever governments tries to do more, the less successful they were. Take economic growth (measure as per capital income) for instance. Within a very short period, the war-ravaged economies of West Germany and Japan made it to the G-7 club and some more are knocking on the door- Taiwan , South Korea, Singapore, Hongkong. Not too far behind are Malaysia, Indonesia and catching up fast are, Thialand, Brazil and Mexico. All these countries have more or less avoided the trap of 'Economic Planning'. In contrast, the tightly regulated economies grew very slowly, if at all , in real terms.

At the dawn of the century, European Russian was more productive and industrially advanced than USA. Today, the productivity there is less than Mexico and Turkey. Before the World War I, Czechoslovakia was more prosperous and industrialised than Germany and France but today it is one of the poorest countries in Europe. China experimented with collective farming, which was a disaster but when privatisation was introduced (in seventies) farm productivity went up by leaps and bounds. After a feverish phase of nationalisations, UK was reduced to the state of the 'sick man of Europe" by the middle seventies. Mrs. Thatcher drastically reduced the government's role and brought about a rapid revival. In India, the productivity of the public sector and returns on the massive investment (to the tune of Rs. 100,000 crores) are very low an it has achieved neither economic nor social objectives. It has also made over private sector less competitive because of the high cost of inputs, which are provided mostly by the governmental monopolies.

Pareto and Inequalities

In the area of taxation and deficit financing also, moderates have generally done much better than the hyperactive. The phenomenon of the 'parallel' economy bears a close association with the taxation levels, even in the developed countries like Italy, Sweden, USA and UK. High tax levels have not contributed significantly to redistribution of incomes but certainly lead to inflation and dishonesty. Generally the outcome of high government spending in inflation and loss of productivity. The empirical evidence suggests that if a greater sector, it leads to higher productivity and wealth generation but in the hands of governments, it mostly gets spent unproductively.

The hyperactive governments do not seem to have made a big dent on inequality either. Even in the egalitarian societies like USSR and China, disparities in income are of a high order. In Western Europe and USA, incomes appear to be distributed more evenly and the levels of absolute poverty are the lowest. In fact, there are many who believe that some of the poverty in countries like USA and UK may be induced by an overdose of social security or welfare doles. Perhaps, the Pareto's law has a lot more validity than what the development economists want us to believe. Pareto concluded that subject to some minor modifications according to prevailing local customs and values, distribution is directly proportionate to an economy's productivity. Less productive the economy, greater is the inequality of income and vice versa.

Poverty Alleviation

In the seventies and the eighties, a substantial and

persuasive body of literature appeared, which focused attention on the issues of re-distributive justice and poverty alleviation. The definition of development in terms of per capita income was broadened to include social indicators such as life expectancy, infant morality and literacy. It was forcefully argued that the benefits of economic progress take in-ordinately long to 'trickle down' to the people below the poverty line and two sets of interventions were advocated. The first called for public intervention assets and incomes in favour of poor and the second aimed at public provision of 'basic needs' such as primary health care; education adult literacy, subsidised food and housing. Governments, particularly in the developing countries, responded by assuming greater responsibilities as provider, and as re-distributors of assets or incomes. Progressive legislation to bring about radical reforms were enacted, private sector was curbed and taxes were raised, in many countries. The public services in health and education expanded to achieve higher coverage of the rural areas. However the results were not uniformly favorable. Countries like Indonesia, Malaysia and Singapore, which achieved substantial reduction in poverty levels, also maintained a high rate of growth and generally did not regulate the economies too tightly. They did not allow taxation levels, deficit financing or public debts to go out of control and similarly kept defence spending and subsidies within reasonable limits. They not only made substantial investments on human resource development but also managed the programmes more efficiently and cost effectively than most other countries. Those who tried to effect transfers in favour of poor by printing more money or by borrowing more or by taxing more were less successful and some pushed the economies to the brink of collapse as a result of reckless and hyperactive policies.

Public Services

Governments have not been able to improve or even maintain quality of services they operate either. Postal services have deteriorated and lagged behind in technology, affording great opportunities for private courier services. Peter Drucker (in his book : The New Realities 1989) has quoted an incident that once Fred Smith, founder and Chief Executive of Federal Express, the multi – national courier company, was asked why his company does not operate in Switzerland. It is the only Western Country he said, 2 in which postal service still functions. Railway, telephones or power generation, have all been less efficient when operated by governments, than in private hands. On one hand, governments have unsuccessfully tried to run services of a commercial nature and on the other, the services which logically should lie in public domain are all deteriorating - whether it be garbage collection or law and order or dispensation of justice.

Reforming Societies

In 'Social Engineering' governments have achieved very little not because of lack of desire but because of intrinsic limitations and choice of unworkable methods. For example prohibition and controlling pronography have been favorite programmes of Governments world over at one time or the other but the policing approach has been given up practically everywhere. In countries like USA, increasingly, legalization of narcotic drugs is being advocated in recognition of the fact that simply outlawing undesirable activities does lead anywhere. Sooner or later, the orthodox abortion of laws in some of the advanced countries are also expected to become more practical. Indian governments, right from the days of the Constituent Assembly, have been very zealous moral crusaders and have attempted to reform the society by enacting laws and getting rid of many social evils like child marriages, dowry, untouchability , caste- system, bigmay etc by the governmental action. The results have been generally poor, although huge amounts have been spent and mammoth bureaucracies have been created to achieve the goals of social engineering. Progressive laws certainly are helpful but when laws are enacted not for enforcing but for projecting a progressive image for short-term political gains, they become irrelevant and ineffectual. What is worse, such laws breed corruption and cynicism. One could apply productive a country is , less are the social inequalities and antiquities.

Management Styles

In the matter of building up human resources by improving health and education, as also in the matter of caring for ill, old, disabled or socially disadvantaged, it is generally recognised that the State has an important role to play and the objectives of the State Policy must be such as would make the society more humane, progressive and harmonious. However the methods of discharging these responsibilities can be markedly different. Channeling more resources in this sector is one part of the task but using them effectively is critically important. An automobile factory, for instance, can either restrict itself to designing, assembling and marketing or buy all components form suppliers or produce everything in house. In practice, it would strike a balance between producing components and services and buying them out. The 'mark-or-buy' options would be constantly reviewed for optimizing profits. Governments can, and often do follow a similar approach. Even in a market economy like USA, the Government accounts for nearly one third of health expenditure and three-fourth of education expenditure but there are very few schools and dispensaries run by the Government. The communities, local self-governing bodies, NGOs and private sector together mange bulk of the social services. Many hyperactive governments, however, try to 'do' things instead of 'getting them done'. The experience in India and many other regulated countries show this approach to be inefficient. Governments often of a step further and try to be an 'ideal' employer. This generally results in excessive employment, high costs, less discipline, less productivity and militant trade unionism in the Government Organisations. The quality and quantity of the output suffer as a natural consequences.

One could argue that government should not actively get involved in such matters. At one time, thinkers like Spencer

Mills and economists like Adam Smith asserted this viewpoint with vigour. In today's context the philosophical or ideological debate is mostly irrelevant. The empirical evidence shows that governments cannot reform societies and therefore, the less energy and money government spend in these efforts, better they would serve the societies.

Bibliography

Adiseshiah, Malcolm S., *Privatisation and State Enterprises*, Calcutta, IIM, 1989.

Agrawal, R C., *State Enterprises in India*, Allahabad, Chaitanya Publishing House, 1961.

Andhra Pradesh Bureau of Economics and Statistics, Brochure on Public Sector Undertakings Andhra Pradesh Owned,Managed and with Shares by the Government of Andhra Pradesh 1969-71 and 1970-71, Hyderabad, 1973.

Andhra Pradesh Bureau of Economics and Statistics, Public Sector Undertakings in Andhra Pradesh: Owned, Managed and with Shares by Govt.of Andhra Pradesh 1967-68 and 1968-69, Hyderabad, 1973.

Andhra Pradesh Bureau of Economics and Statistics, *Report on the Performance of State Public Sector Non-Departmental Undertakings for the Years 1982-83 to 1985-86 in Andhra Pradesh*, Hyderabad, 1989.

Andhra Pradesh Department of Public Enterprises, Andhra Pradesh Public Enterprises: Performance 1992-93, Hyderabad, Department of Public Enterprises.

Andhra Pradesh Department of Public Enterprises, *Andhra Pradesh State Public Enterprises Performance 1987-88*, Hyderabad, Govt. Central Press, 1989.

Andhra Pradesh Department of Public Enterprises, Andhra

Pradesh State Public Enterprises: Performance 1989-90, Hyderabad, n.p.

Andhra Pradesh Department of Public Enterprises, Andhra Pradesh State public enterprises performance 1990-91, Hyderabad, Department of Public Enterprises, n.d.

Andhra Pradesh Department of Public Enterprises, Andhra Pradesh State Public Enterprises: Performance 1988-89, Hyderabad, Department of Public Enterprises, 1989.

Andhra Pradesh Department of Public Enterprises, Andhra Pradesh State Public Enterprises: Performance 1991-92, Hyderabad, Department of Public Enterprises, 1992.

Andhra Pradesh Department of Public Enterprises, Background papers for draft white paper on public enterprises, Hyderabad, DPE, 1989.

Andhra Pradesh Industrial Development Corporation Limited, *Andhra Pradesh Industrial Development Corporation Limited: Projects under implementation.*

Andhra Pradesh Public Enterprise Management Board, Andhra Pradesh State Public Enterprises: Performance During 1986-87, Hyderabad.

Andhra Pradesh Public Enterprise Management Board, Andhra Pradesh State Public Enterprises: Performance During 1984-85, Hyderabad.

Andhra Pradesh Public Enterprise Management Board, Andhra Pradesh State Public Enterprises: Performance during 1985-86, Hyderabad, PENB, 1986.

Andhra Pradesh Public Enterprises Management Board, *Andhra Pradesh State Public Enterprises: Performance during 1986-87*, Hyderabad.

Andhra Pradesh Public Enterprises Management Board, Andhra Pradesh State Public Enterprises: Performance during 1985-86, Hyderabad.

Andhra Pradesh Public Enterprises Management Board,

Performance of A P State Public Enterprises During 1985-86, Hyderabad.

Andhra Pradesh, *State Level Conference of Public Enterprises 11th April 1988*, Technical Session-1: Background Papers.

Appa Rao, B., *Small enterprise promotion in Andhra Pradesh: Role of Andhra Pradesh State Financial Corporation.*

Assam Department of Public Enterprises, Annual Report of State Public Enterprises in Assam 1980-81 to 1986-87, Guwahati, Assam Govt. Press, 1990.

Basu, S K and Sarkar, A and Sinha, H N., *Report on the Monetary and Non-Monetary Work Incentives in Public Enterprises of West Bengal*, Calcutta, Book Exchange, 1971.

Batra, Satish K (Ed.) and Jain, Tej K (Ed.), *State Enterprises: The Emerging Scenario*, Jaipur, Printwell Publishers, 1988.

Bhambhri, C P., *Parliamentary Control over state Enterprise in India*, Delhi, Metropolitian Book Co, 1960.

Bhandari, K C., Nationalisation of industries in India, Calcutta, Academic Press, 1962.

Bhanu Prasad Committee, *Management of State Level Public Enterprises: Report.*

Bhat, K S and Nandagopal, R., Role of Chairman and Managing Directors in State Level Public Enterprises: A Discussion, Hyderabad, IPE, 1991.

Bhatra, G S., *Leading Issues in Public Enterprises: Control and Accountability*, New Delhi, Anmol, 1993.

Capoor, H K L (Chairman), India Ministry of Home Affairs Department of Personnel and Administrative Reforms, *Report of the Standing Group on Management of Public Enterprises in the States*, New Delhi, Govt.of India Press, 1979.

Chauhan, *Organisation and Working of Public Enterprises in Gujarat*, Vallabh Vidyanagar, Sardar Patel University, 1978, viii, 580p. Rs.28.

Chinta Rao, N., *Working Capital Management:(A Study of Selected State Enterprises of Karnataka)*, Nagarjuna Nagar, Nagarjuna University, 1988.

Damodar Dass, C., *Study of Performance Improvement in APSRTC through Computerised Maintenance Management*, Hyderabad, IPE, 1993.

Diwakar Rao, P L (Ed), *Public Sector in Andhra Pradesh : A Handbook & Directory*, Sec'bad.

Diwakar Rao, P L (ED), *Public Sector in Andhra Pradesh: A Handbook and Directory*, Secunderabad, 1988.

Diwakar Rao, P L (Ed.), Public sector in Andhra Pradesh, Secunderabad, Utility Publications, 1988.

Diwakar Rao, P L (Ed.), *Public Sector in Andhra Pradesh: A Handbook and Directory* (With Special Supplement on Central Sector).

Dutt, R C., *State Enterprises in a Developing Country: The Indian Experience 1950-90*, New Delhi, Abhinav Publications, 1990.

Dutta, Abhijit., *Privatisation of Public Enterprises: An Empirical Study Relating to Some Selected Privatised SLPEs in Orissa*, Bhubaneswar, Utkal University, 1995.

Gavini, Augustine L., Ancillaries of Public Enterprises in Andhra Pradesh-A Study in Structure, Growth and Performance, Hyderabad, O U, 1990.

Gorwala, A D., India Planning Commission, Report on the Efficient Conduct of State Enterprises, New Delhi, 1951.

Gowri Sankar Rao, P., *State Level Public Enterprises of Kerala*: (A Study on the Problems of Financial Management). Nagarjuna Nagar, Nagarjuna Univ., 1989.

Gujarat Bureau of Public Enterprises, *Public Enterprises Eighth Annual Report 1984-85*, Gandhinagar, 1987.

Gujarat Bureau of Public Enterprises, *Public Enterprises Fifth Annual Report 1981-82*, Gandhinagar, Govt. Central Press, 1983.

Gujarat Bureau of Public Enterprises, *Public Enterprises Sixth Annual Report 1982-83*, Gandhinagar, 1984.

Gujarat Bureau of Public Enterprises, *Public Sector Enterprises Fourth Annual Report 1980-81*, Gandhinagar, Govt. Central Press.

Gujarat Bureau of Public Enterprises, Public Sector Enterprises Fourth Annual Report 1980-81, Gandhinagar, Govt.Central Press.

Gujarat State Road Transport Corporation, Statistics of GSRT Corporation, Ahmedabad

Gupta, Nirmal K. and Ahmad, Abad. *Management Research: Contemporary Issues*, Delhi, South Asia Publications, 1994.

Gupta, Shah, *Financial Working of Public Utilities*, Jaipur, Printwell, 1992.

Guptha, G C., Role of Andhra Pradesh Enterprises Management Board-A Critical Appraisal, Hyderabad, IPE, 1986.

Hassan, Shabir, *Public Enterprises in Economic Development*, Delhi, Amol Publications Pvt. Ltd., 1987.

Hemlata Rao, *Financial Performance of Public Enterprises*, Jaipur, Printwell Publishers, 1987.

India Comptroller and Auditor General, Digest of important observations by the Comptroller and Auditor General of India on the performance of the State Electricity Boards 1980-85, New Delhi, Indian Audit and Accounts Department, 1987.

India Comptroller and Auditor General, Report of the Comptroller and Auditor General of India for the Year Ended 31 March 1989 No.4 (Commercial) of Government of Andhra Pradesh: Andhra Pradesh State Civil Supplies Corporation Limited and Andhra Pradesh State Essential Commodities Corportion Limited, Hyderabad, Govt. Central Press, 1991.

India Comptroller and Auditor General, State government public enterprises - concepts, performance and accountability, New Delhi, Indian Audit and Accounts Department, 1989, v, 220p.

India, Comptroller and Auditor General, *Report of the Comptroller and Auditor General of India*, (Commercial) Government of Punjab, Chandigarh, Controller of Printing & Stationery.

India, Comptroller and Auditor General, *Report of the Comptroller and Auditor General of India of Union Government No.6* (Commercial) of 1990: Delhi Transport Corporation, Delhi, Controller of Publications, 1991.

India, Maharashtra, *Performance of State Public Enterprises-1994-95*, Mumbai, Government Press , 1996.

Institute of Public Enterprise, Andhra Pradesh Public Enterprise Yearbook 1984, Hyderabad, 1984.

Institute of Public Enterprise, Colloquium on State Level Public Enterprises: June 25-26, 1982, Hyderabad, IPE, 1982.

Institute of Public Enterprise, Course Material on Finance and Accounting, Hyderabad, IPE, 1991.

Institute of Public Enterprise, Course on Project Appraisal for State Level Public Enterprises in Karnataka, Hyderabad, IPE, 1984.

Institute of Public Enterprise, Management Development Programme for Young Executives from APSLPEs - Phase-I (APPEMB): 27-10-92 to 31-10-92, Hyderabad, IPE, 1992.

Institute of Public Enterprise, National Seminar on PE Reform and Privatisation in State Level Public Enterprises: Strategies and Techniques, Hyderabad, IPE, 1992.

Institute of Public Enterprise, One Week Course on SLPE Management: 1-6 February, 1988, Hyderabad, IPE, 1988.

Institute of Public Enterprise, One Week Course on State Level Public Enterprises Management for IAS Officers: June 13-18, 1988, Hyderabad, IPE, 1988.

Institute of Public Enterprise, One-Week Programme on SLPEs: 24-29 October, 1988, Hyderabad, IPE, 1988.

Institute of Public Enterprise, Privatisation: Reorientation of State Level Public Enterprises: August 24-28, 1992, Hyderabad, IPE, 1992.

Institute of Public Enterprise, Programme on Budget and Budgetary Control for Executives of AP SLPEs: 25-27 April, 1985, Hyderabad, IPE, 1985.

Institute of Public Enterprise, Programme on Corporate Planning in SLPEs: Sponsored by Department of Public Enterprises and Government of Andhra Pradesh, Hyderabad, IPE, 1991.

Institute of Public Enterprise, Programme on Management of SLPEs: March 6-11, 1989, Hyderabad, IPE, 1989.

Institute of Public Enterprise, Programme on Management of SLPEs: 19-24 June, 1989, Hyderabad, IPE, 1989.

Institute of Public Enterprise, Programme on Management of SLPEs: 10-15 July, 1989, Hyderabad, IPE, 1989.

Institute of Public Enterprise, Programme on Management of State Level Public Enterprises: 22-28 August, 1988, Hyderabad, IPE, 1988.

Institute of Public Enterprise, Programme on Management of State Level Public Enterprises Level II: 7-12 August, 1989, Hyderabad, IPE, 1989.

Institute of Public Enterprise, Programme on Management of State Level Public Enterprises Level II: 21-26 August, 1989, Hyderabad, IPE, 1989.

Institute of Public Enterprise, Programme on Problem Solving Based Training for SLPE Managers: 23-27 October, 1989, Hyderabad, IPE, 1989.

Institute of Public Enterprise, Programme on Working Capital Management for Executives of State Level Public Enterprises of N E Region: 18-23 January, 1990, Hyderabad, IPE, 1990.

Institute of Public Enterprise, Report on Financial Performance of State Level Public Enterprises in India (1980-81 to 1985-86): Statistical Statement, Hyderabad, IPE, 1991.

Institute of Public Enterprise, Top Management Programme for SLPE's in North Eastern Region: February 20-24, 1989, Hyderabad, IPE, 1989.

Institute of Public Enterprise, Workshop on Project Appraisal for SLPEs: August 22-26, 1983, Hyderabad, IPE, 1983.

Institute of Public Enterprise, Workshop on SLPEs: October 7, 1988, Hyderabad, IPE, 1988.

Jain, Ravi K., *Working Capital Management of State Enterprises in India*. Jaipur, National Publishing House, 1988.

Jessica, Mary V., *Performance of state financial corporations: A study of APSFC and KSFC*, Hyderabad, O U, 1992.

Karnataka Electricity Board, *Pocket-Book of Electricity Statistics 1979*, Bangalore, 1979.

Karnataka State Bureau of Public Enterprises, *Public Sector Enterprises First Annual Report*, Bangalore, n.d.

Karnataka State Bureau of Public Enterprises, *Public Sector Enterprises Second Annual Report 1981-82*, Bangalore , n.d.

Kerala Bureau of Public Enterprises and Centre for Management Development, Review of Public Enterprises in Kerala, Trivandrum, 1995-96.

Kerala, *A Review of Public Enterprises in Kerala*, Thiruvanthapuram, Govt. Press, 1998.

Kiran Kumar, K., Cash Management in Selected State Level Manufacturing Public Enterprises in Andhra Pradesh: Thesis Submitted to the Osmania University for the Award of Doctor of Philosophy in Commerce, Hyderabad, Osmania University, 1990.

Kolekar, B D., Human resources development: A study of selected public undertakings in Maharashtra and Goa, New Delhi, Northern Book Centre, 1993.

Kumara Swamy, V., *Study of Rajahansa Services in Hyderabad City Transport*, Hyderabad, IPE, 1993.

Maharashtra State Bureau of Public Enterprises, *Performance of State Public Enterprises (1989-90)*, Bombay, Govt. Central Press, 1991.

Maharashtra State Bureau of Public Enterprises, Performance of State Public Enterprises (1989-90), Bombay, Govt.Central Press, 1991.

Maharashtra State Bureau of Public Enterprises, Performance of State Public Sector Enterprises (1987-88), Bombay, Central Govt. Press, 1989.

Maharashtra State Bureau of Public Enterprises, Performance of state public enterprises 1992-93, Government of Maharashtra, Bombay, Government Central Press, 1994.

Maharashtra State Bureau of Public Enterprises, Performance of state public enterprises 1991-92, Government of Maharashtra, Bombay, Government Central Press, 1992.

Maharashtra State Bureau of Public Sector Enterprises, Performance of State Public Sector Enterprises (1986-87), Bombay, Govt.Central Press, 1988.

Maharashtra State Road Transport Corporation, *Twenty Five Years of State Transport: Maharashtra*, Bombay, 1974.

Maharashtra, *Performance of State Public Enterprises 1995-96*, Mumbai, Govt. Press, 1998.

Maharashtra, Performance of State Public Enterprises 1996-97, Mumbai, Govt. Press, 1998.

Maruthi Ram, P., Financing of Public Enterprises - a study of the impact on cost of Funds in select Central Enterprises and Andhra Pradesh Government Hyderabad, Osmania University, 1987.

Mathur, B. L. (Ed.), Organisation and management of public enterprises. Vol.III, Performance evaluation of public enterprises, Jaipur, Arihant. 996.

Mathur, D C., *Wages in the Public Sector (A Study of Rajasthan State Enterprises)*, New Delhi, Mittal Publications, 1990.

Minhas, Anil and Singh, Amrik and Chumber, Gurbax Ram and Chanana, Sanjeev, Financial Committees at State Level, New Delhi, Deep & Deep Publications, 1990.

Mishra, R K and Nandagopal R and Suri Babu, P (Study Team), Institute of Public Enterprise, Study report on financial contribution and requirements of state level public enterprises in India. 2 Vols., Hyderabad, IPE, 1993.

Mishra, R K and Nandagopal, R (Study Team), Institute of Public Enterprise, Financial performance of state level public enterprises in India, Hyderabad, IPE, 1990.

Mishra, R K and Nandagopal, R (Study Team), Institute of Public Enterprise, Budgeting in state level public enterprises in Andhra Pradesh and Tamil Nadu, Hyderabad, IPE, 1991.

Mishra, R K and Nandagopal, R., *State Level Public Enterprises in Bihar*, Hyderabad, IPE, 1990.

Mishra, R K and Pakki Reddy, G., *Role of Public Enterprises in the Financing of the Seventh Plan: a case of the State Level Public Enterprises in Andhra Pradesh*, Hyderabad.

Mishra, R K and Ravishankar, S and Nandagopal, R (Eds.), *Management of State Level Public Enterprises in India*, New Delhi, National Publishing House, 1989.

Mishra, R K and RaviShankar, S., *Capacity utilisation in State Level Public Enterprises in Andhra Pradesh*, Institute of Public Enterprise, Hyderabad, 1987.

Mishra, R.K., and Pakki Reddy, G., *Technical Note on the State Level Public Enterprises in Andhra Pradesh*, Hyderabad, IPE, 1988.

Mohammed, Latif Syed A., Performance of joint sector enterprises promoted by selected SIDCs: (A study of objectives, management and financial performance), Hyderabad, Osmania University, 1992.

Murthy, K S N., *Industrial Relations in Andhra Pradesh State Electricity Board*, Hyderabad, IPE, 1985.

Nandagopal, R and Vudali, Mohan V K., *Internal Audit in SLPEs of Andhra Pradesh*, Institute of Public Enterprise, Hyderabad, 1991.

Narayana Murty, A S Y., *Project Report on Industrial Sickness-causes and cures (a study in APSFC's experience)*, Hyderabad, IPE, 1984.

Omprakash, *Theory and Working of State Corporations: With Special Reference to India*, London, George Allen and Unwin Ltd., 1962.

Orissa Department of Public Enterprises, Public enterprises profile 1989-90, Government of Orissa, Cuttack, Government Press, 1990.

Orissa Planning and Coordination Department, Compilation of Circulars Relating to the State Public Sector Undertakings (Compiled upto the 30th April,1980),1966.

Orissa Planning and Coordination Department, *Public Enterprises Profile 1985-86 compiled up to 31-3-1986*, Cuttack, Govt. Press, 1987.

Orissa Planning and Coordination Department, *Public Enterprises Profile 1986-87 compiled up to 31-3-1987*, Cuttack, Govt. Press, 1988.

Orissa Planning and Coordination Department, *Public Enterprises Profile 1987-88* (Compiled upto 31-3-1988), Cuttack, Govt. Press, 1989.

Parathasarathy, R (Consultant), Institute of Public Enterprise, Study of Wages of and other Monetary and Non-Monetary Benefits and Concession given to the Employees of Andhra Pradesh State, Tamilnadu, Karnataka, Madhya Pradesh and Maharashtra State Electricity Boards, Hyderabad, IPE

Prasad Rao, P., Management Audit for State Level Public Enterprises: A Case Study of Leather Industry Development Corporation, Hyderabad, IPE, 1991.

Punjab Bureau of Public Enterprises, Second Report on the Working of State Public Sector Undertakings 1980-81, Chandigarh, Govt.Press, 1981.

Punjab Bureau of Public Enterprises, Sixth Report on the Working of State Public Sector Undertakings 1986-87.

Rajasthan Bureau of Public Enterprises, *Public Enterprises Profile 1986-87*, Jaipur, Govt. Central Press, 1988.

Rajasthan Bureau of Public Enterprises, *Public Enterprises Profile 1984-85*, Jaipur, Govt. Central Press, 1986.

Rajasthan Bureau of Public Enterprises, *Public Enterprises Profile*, Jaipur, Govt. Central Press, 1985.

Rajasthan Bureau of Public Enterprises, *Public Enterprises Profile 1983-84*, Jaipur, Govt. Central Press, 1985.

Rajasthan Bureau of Public Enterprises, *Public Enterprises Profile 1984-85*, Jaipur, Govt. Central Press, 1986.

Rajasthan Bureau of Public Enterprises, *Public Enterprises Profile 1986-87*, Jaipur, Govt.Central Press, 1988.

Rajasthan Bureau of Public Enterprises, Public Enterprises Profile 1988-89.

Rajasthan Bureau of Public Enterprises, *Public Sector Undertakings at a Glance 1982*. Jaipur, 1982.

Ramamurti, Ravi (Ed.) and Vernon, Raymond (Ed.), Privatization and Control of State-Owned Enterprises, Washington, 1991.

Raman Rao, T V., *Industrial relations in Andhra Pradesh State Electricity Board*.

Roy, R C., *State Public Enterprise in India*, New Delhi, Uppal Publishing House, 1985.

Sai Baba, P., *Cost Control and Cost Reduction in a State Transport Undertaking: a case study of APSRTC*, Hyderabad, IPE, 1988.

Sankar, T L and Mishra, R K and Nanda Gopal, R., *Can State Level Public Enterprises in India Earn a Rate of Return?* Bombay, 1990.

Sankar, T L and Mishra, R K and Nanda Gopal, R., *Working of State-Level Manufacturing Public Enterprises: Promise and Performance*, Hyderabad, IPE, 1991.

Sankar, T L and Nanda Gopal, R and Mishra, R K., *State Level Public Enterprises in India: An Overview*, Bombay, 1990.

Sankar, T L and Nandagopal, R and Mishra, R K., *Performance and Development of State Level Public Enterprises in India*, Hyderbad, IPE, 1989.

Sankar, T L and Nandagopal, R and Mishra, R K., *Performance and Development of State Level Public Enterprises in India*, Hyderabad, IPE, 1989.

Sankar, T L and Nandagopal, R and Mishra, R K., *State Level Public Enterprises in India: an overview*, Institute of Public Enterprise, Hyderabad, 1989.

Sankar, T L and Parathasarathy, R (Study Team), Institute of Public Enterprise, Study of wages and other monetary and non-monetary benefits and concessions given to the employees of Andhra Pradesh State, Tamil Nadu, Karnataka, Madhya Pradesh and Maharashtra State Electricity Boards. 2 Vols., Hyderabad, IPE, 1990.

Sankar, T L and Santana Babu, G and Trivikram, K (Study Team), Institute of Public Enterprise, Andhra Pradesh State Textile Development Corporation: A study, Hyderabad, IPE, 1982.

Sankar, T L, Institute of Public Enterprise, Management of state level public enterprises and its privatisation, Hyderabad, IPE, 1993.

Sankar, T. L. and Nandagopal, R and Mishra, R K., *Management of State Level Public Enterprises in India*, Jaipur, Printwell, 1992.

Saraswathy Rao, Y., *Public Enterprises: A State Level Perspective*, Delhi, B.R.Publishing Company, 1986.

Sarma, R P., *Investment Pattern of Public Undertakings in India: A Study of Orissa Enterprises*, Delhi, Mittal Publications, 1987.

Sarma, S D., *Study of Project Appraisal Systems in Financial Institutions with special reference to APSFC*, Hyderabad, IPE, 1985.

Satish Chander, T., Legislative control over corporate sector, Jaipur, RBSA, 1994.

Satyanarayana, J., *Working of the Andhra Pradesh State Road Transport Corporation*, New Delhi, Concept Publishing Co., 1985.

Selvarani, S., *Employees Welfare Measures in Select Public Enterprises in Andhra Pradesh*, Hyderabad, O U, 1993.

Sharma, G D., *Working of State Enterprises in Rajasthan*, New Delhi, Sterling Publishers Pvt. Ltd., 1975.

Shirley, Mary M., Managing State-Owned Enterprises, Washington, World Bank, 1983.

Shirley, Mary M., World Bank, Managing State-owned Enterprises, Washington, 1983.

Shiva Ramu, S., *State Eneterprises in Karnataka: An Introduction to State Intervention*, Bangalore, IIM-B, 1983.

Shiva Ramu, S., *State Enterprises in Karnataka: an Introduction to State Intervention*, Bangalore, IIM, 1983.

Simha, S L N., Development Banking in India with Special Reference to a State Level Institution-Karnataka, Madras, Institute for Financial Management and Research, 1976.

Singh, Mohinder, *Some aspects of public enterprises in India.*

Singh, Nagendra P., *Financial Management in State Enterprises (A Case Study of Bihar State Road Transport Corporation)*, Delhi, Capital Publishing House, 1989.

State Level Conference of Chairman and Chief Executives Enterprises (11-4-1988), State Level Conference of Chairman and Chief Executives Enterprises (11-4-1988), n.p., 1988.

Sujatha Rao, T., *Annotated Bibliography on Public Enterprise in India*, Hyderabad, IPE, 1994, 753p.

Suryanaranaya, M., *Monograph on Andhra Pradesh State Financial Corporation a catalyst of Industrial Development in Andhra Pradesh*, Hyderabad, IPE, 1986.

Swamy, K., *Financial Performance of Manufacturing State Level Public Enterprises in Andhra Pradesh*, Hyderabad, JNTU, 1992.

Swamy, K., *Financial Performance of Manufacturing State Level Public Enterprises*, Delhi, Delta Publishing House, 1994.

Tamil Nadu Bureau of Public Enterprises, *Review of Public Sector Enterprises in Tamilnadu 1979-80*, Madras, Tamil Arasu Press.

Tamil Nadu Bureau of Public Enterprises, Review of state public sector enterprises in Tamilnadu 1986-87, Madras, Govt. Central Press.

Tamil Nadu Finance Department, *Review of Public Sector Enterprises in Tamil Nadu 1976-77*, Madras, 1978.

Tamil Nadu State Bureau of Public Enterprises, *Handbook of Instruction for State Public Sector Undertakings and Statutory Boards*, Madras.

Tandon, B C., *Public Enterprises in India*, Allahabad, Chaitanya Publishing House, 1987.

TZE, Ker Sin, *Public Enterprises in Asia; An introductory Survey*, Singapore, Institute of Southeast Asian Studies, 1978.

Umesh, D., *Identification of Market Segment for APTEX Shirts*, Hyderabad, IPE, 1993.

Uttar Pradesh Bureau of State Enterprises, Annual Report on the Working of UP State Enterprises 1978-79, Allahabad, Superintendent of Printing and Stationery, 1981.

Vanamala, M., *Public Sector Enterprises: An Enquiry into the Corporations for Weaker Sections in Andhra Pradesh*, Anantapur, Sri Krishna Devaraya Univ., 1989.

Vananamala, M and Pakki Reddy, G and Uma Shankari, P and Rasool Saheb, T S (Study Team), Institute of Public

Enterprise, Contributions of public enterprises to economic development of Andhra Pradesh (Sponsored by Department of Finance, Government of Andhra Pradesh) 2 Vols., Hyderabad, IPE, 1984.

Vasanth Kumar, R., *Study of the Over-run in Projects Promoted by APSFC*, Hyderabad, IPE, 1993.

Venkatswamy, G., *Management of State Government Enterprises in Andhra Pradesh*. n.p, 1984.

Venkatswamy, G., *Management of State Government Enterprises*, New Delhi, Archives Publishers, 1987.

Vuylsteke, Charles and Nankani, Helen, World Bank, *Techniques of Privatization of State-owned Enterprises*, 3 vols, Vol.I - Report on techniques of privatization and related issues. Vol.II - Country and case studies. Vol.III - Bibliography and other reference material, Washington, 1988.

Index

A

ACC Ltd., 72, 73

Action Plan, 104, 134

Agro-Industrial Production, 145

AIDMK Led Govt., 62

All States Network, 42

All States Total Revenue Earned, 43

Allahabad High Court, 74

Allwyn Nissan, 88

Andhra Pradesh, 3-5, 147, 149, 151, 152, 154

APSLPEs (Andhra Pradesh SLPEs), 194

Arjun Sengupta Committee, 190, 196

Arunachal Pradesh, 4

Assam, 4-6, 147, 149

Assembly Elections, 82

Auto Tractors Ltd., (ATL), 66, 75-77, 79-81, 84, 85

Autonomy, 109

B

Balance Useful Life Method, 71

Bigamy, 203

Bihar, 145, 147, 149

Bikaner Woolens Mills, 102

Billimoria & Co., 70, 72, 84

BJP Led Govt., 62

Bombay Stock Exchange, 64

Book Depreciation Method, 71

Bureau of Private Enterprises, (BPE), 103, 104

Bureau of State Public Enterprises, (BSPE), 123, 124

Bureau's Advisory Board, 119

C

CAG India, 3, 62

Capital Employed, 40

Capital Market, 56

Capitalization, 91, 93

Caste System, 203

Central Public Enterprise Sector, 144

Central Public Enterprises, 1, 2, 188

Central Public Sector Undertakings, 98, 105

Central Public Sectors, 98

Child Marriages, 203

China, 200

Chunar, 67-69, 72

Chunar Plants, 71
CIDCO, 112
Collective Farming, 200
Commercial Enterprises, 112
Communist and Socialist Models, 199
Communist Central Planning, (USSR and Eastern Europe), 199
Companies Act, 1956, 108, 131, 144, 55, 59, 60, 98, 110
Congress (I) Led Govt., 621
Controller of Capital Issues India, 93
Cooperative Societies Act, 1965, 98, 144, 153
Corporate
  Autonomy, 189
  Management, 197
  Plan, 104
  Planning, 134
Czechoslovakia, 200

D

Dalmias, 72-75, 82, 84
Dalmias Industries, 73
Deficit Financing, 201, 202
Delhi, 3, 6
Depreciation Policy, 89
Developing Countries, 84, 201, 202
Diversification and Modernization, 52
Dowry, 203

E

Economic and Social Infrastructure, 4
Economic Development, 48, 101
Economic Growth, 198, 200
Economic Planning, 199, 200
Economic Policy, 49
Economic Structure, 154
Economy, 66
Education, 199
Education Adult Literacy, 202
Egalitarian Societies, 201
Eighth Plan, 48
Expert Committee, 79

F

Financial Autonomy, 135
Financial Institutions, 98, 125
Financial Markets, 84
Financial Resources, 111, 125
Five Year Plan, 134
Forest Dev. Corp., 151
Free Market Economy, 199
FSLPEs (Financial State Level Public Enterprises), 150

G

GDP (Gross Domestic Product), 1
Germany and France, 200
Goa, 5
GSDP, (Gross State Domestic Product), 1
Gujarat, 3-5, 146, 147, 149, 154

H

Haffkins Bio Pharmaceutical Corp., 112
HAL, 87-89, 91, 94, 96
Handloom and Handicraft Corp., 150
Haryana, 5

Heavy Industries, 194
Himachal Pradesh, 4, 145
Hindustan Zinc, 103
Hire and Fire Policies, 53
Hitachi Japan, 88
Hong Kong, 200
Hyderabad Allwyn, 86

I

India, 90
Indian Constitution, 60
Indian Economy, 48
Indian Public Enterprises, 52
Indicative Planning, (France and Japan), 199
Indonesia, Malaysia and Singapore, 202
Industrial Dev. Bank of India, 151
Industrial Development Corp., 150
Industrial Development, 145
Industrial Enterprises, 66
Industrial Project Proposals, 133
Industrialization, 3, 150
Informational Development, 199
Infrastructure Services, 4
Instrumentation Ltd. Kota, 102
Italy—UK, 201

J

Jammu and Kashmir, 5, 6, 147
Japan, 200
JD Led Govt., 62
Joint Sector Companies, 144

K

Kanoria Industries, 79
Kapoor Committee, 190
Karnataka, 3, 4, 147, 149
Kerala, 4-6, 144, 147, 149
Konarak TV, 134
Kothari Directory, 65
Krishna Engineering, 194
Krishna Menon Committee, 190

L

Legal System, 60
Leyland Motors, 76, 79
List of PSUs, 140-142
  Classification, 142
  Commercial, 142
  Financial, 142
  Promotions, 142

M

Madhya Pradesh, 4-6
Maharashtra, 3-5,146, 147, 149, 151, 154
  Oil Seeds Commercial and Industrial Corp., 114
  State Electricity Board (MSEB), 108, 111
  State Financial Corp., 112
  State Road Transport Corp., 111, 113
  State Textile Corp., 112
  State Warehousing Corp., 112
Mahindra and Mahindra, 88
Malaysia, 200
Management Information Systems, 189
Management Reforms, 196
Market Economy (USSR, EEC Countries), 199
Medium and Small Industries, 150

Meghalaya and Orissa, 154
Mexico, 200
Mitsubishi, 88
Mizoram, 4, 6
MoU, 46, 47, 52, 53, 133-135, 196, 197
Mrs. Thatcher, 200
MSLPES (Manufacturing State Level Public Enterprise), 147, 148
Mutual Funds, 63

N

Nagaland, 5
Narcotic Drugs, 203
NCAER (National Council of Applied Eco. Res.), 104
Ninth Finance Commission, 112
Ninth Plan, 3
Non-Governmental Organizations, 204
Non-Industrial Sector, 52
Non-Privatization Reforms, 188

O

OPTIMA (Optimum Performance Through Internal Mgmt. Action), 47, 53
Orissa Agro Industrial Corp., 134
Orissa, 4, 6, 147
  Forest Dev. Corp., 134
  Industrial Development Corp., 134
  Mining Corp., 134
  Mining Deposits, 136
  Power Generation Corp., 134
  State Electronic Dev. Corp., 134
  State Housing Board, 134
  State Plantation Dev. Corp., 134
  State Road Transport Corp., 134
Overseas Employment and Export Promotion Corp., 114

P

Pareto's Law, 201
Patel Industries, 79
Performance Evaluation System, 53
Planning
  Commission, 1-3, 109
  Era, 97
  Models, 198
  Corporate, 55
  Production, 55
  Strategic, 55
Political Party, 2
Pondicherry, 4, 5
Power Commission, 61
Price Earning Ratio Methods, 64
Primary Health Care, 202
Private Sector, 52, 56, 59, 60, 87, 89, 91, 96, 99, 102, 103, 124, 125, 148, 202, 204
Privatization, 48, 49, 52, 56, 60-63, 65, 82-84, 86, 87, 199, 200
  and Non-Privatization Reforms, 143
  Classification and Methods, 57
  Modalities, 56, 57, 59
  Private Placement, 56
  Projects, 86
  Program, 65
  Public Floatation, 56, 57
  Trade Sale,
Project Approval Committees, 133

Projects Contents, 125
Projects Reforms, 125
Prominent Enterprises in Rajasthan, 100
Promotional Enterprises, 4
Promotional SLPEs, 151
Provident Fund, 60, 63
PSLPEs, 152
  Number, 152
Public Corporations, 52
Public Enterprises, 3, 48, 49, 53, 60, 66, 69, 115, 124, 127
  Accounting System, 128
  Classification, 115-121
  Costing System, 129
  Department.of-, 133
  In Rajasthan, 99, 105-107
  Internal Audit, 129
  Management Information System, 129
  Organization Structure, 126
  Performance and Evaluation System, 128
  Personal Policies, 127
  Recruitment Policies, 127
  Reforms, 45
  Role, 124
  System in India, 1, 48
Public Sector, 51, 97, 199
Public Sector Enterprises, 101, 108, 109, 112-114
  Classification, 108
  Composition Fin. Resources, 111
  in Maharashtra, 108
Public Sector Reforms in Rajasthan, 97
Public Sector Undertakings, 131, 134
  Commercial, 141
  Functioning, 133
  Role as Employment Agency, 133
Public State Undertakings, 131
Punjab, 3, 149

R

Rajadhyaksha, VG, 109
Rajasthan, 3-5, 98, 105, 145, 147
  Chemical Works, 103
  Coop. Marketing Federation, 102
  Development and Investment Corp., 99
  Finance Corp., 99
  Housing Board, 99
  Land Development Corp., 103
  Rajya Van Vikas Nigam, 102
  State Agro Industries Corp., 102
  State Coop. Oil Seeds Growers Federation, 102
  State Cooperative Marketing Corp., 103
  State Electricity Board, 99, 100
  State Hotel Corp., 103
  State Mineral Corp., 103
  State Road Transport Corp., 103
  State Tanneries, 102
  Tourist Development Corp., 103
Raunaq Industries, 79
Raymond Woolens, 72
Reforming Societies, 203
Reforms, 87
Reforms and Privatization, 97
Reforms in State Public Sector Undertakings, 1-3
Republic Forge, AP, 194
Resource Generation, 162
Resource Mobilization, 46, 47, 55

Revenue Expenditure, 126
Road Transport Corp., 196

S

Sales Tax, 74
SC, ST and OBCs, 194
Scheduled Caste and Scheduled Tribes, 4, 153
Scheduled Caste Development, 98
Sectors, 66
  Agro-Processing Industry, 66
  Engineering, 87
  Infrastructure, 66
  Mining or Construction, 66
  Public, 102, 103, 104
Seiko Japan, 88
Sick Industrial Companies (Spl. Provision) Act, 114
SICOM, 112
Similiphar Forest Dev. Corp., 134
Singapore, 200
Sipani Automobiles, 79-81, 83, 87
Sixth Five Year Plan, 143
SLPEs (State Level Public Enterprises), 1-4, 45, 46, 48, 49, 51-57, 59-62, 63, 65, 86, 87, 96, 97, 99, 105, 108, 133, 134, 143-149, 153, 188-191, 193-197
  Classification, 49
  Divisions, 146
  Financial Performance, 2, 145
  In Maharashtra, 108
  Privatisation of-, 45
  Profile, 143
  Reforms, 48
  State-wise List of-, 39
  System, 144
  Total Involvement, 3
Small Industrial and Tourism, 145
Small Industries Corp., 102
Social Engineering, 203
Social Security, 199
Social Services Sector, 199
Socialist Mixed Economic Planning (India etc), 199
Society, 4, 145, 154
  Backward Class of-, 4
Socio-Economic Upliftment, 154
Sodium Sulphate Plant, 103
South Korea, 199, 200
State Bureau of Public Enterprise, 109
State Bureau of Public State Enterprises, 110
State Dairy Development Corporation, 54
State Electricity Boards (SEB), 4, 61, 144, 193, 196
State Electricity Development Corporation, 54
State Enterprises, 81
State Policy, 204
State Public Enterprises, 97-101, 98, 99
  Guidelines-, (Mah), 122
  Sectoral Composition, 98
State Public Sector Undertakings in Orissa, 131
State Public Sectors, 1-2, 104
State Road Transport Corp., 4, 61, 144
State's Economy, 97
State-wise
  Capital Investment in SLPEs, 158

Financial Performance of
SLPEs, 160
Gowth of SLPEs during Plans,
156

T

Taiwan, 199, 200
Tamil Nadu, 3-6, 146, 147, 151
Taxation, 201
Technical Collaboration
Agreement, 76
Telecom Industry, 6
Telecommunication and Banking,
136
Thailand, Brazil, 200
Top Ten Loss Enterprises, 165
Top Ten Profit Enterprises, 165
Total Investment in State, 40
Tourism, 97
Tourism Dev. Corp., 151
Tourism Development
Enterprises, 152
Trade and Marketing, 145
Trading and Services Enterprises,
3, 4
Transfer of Ownership, 85
Transparency, 48, 65, 83, 86, 87,
196
Tribal Area Development, 98
Tribal Development Corp., 112
Tribal Population, 152
Tripura, 145
TSLPEs (Trade and Services
SLPEs), 148, 149
Turkey, 200

U

United Kingdom, 90, 200, 201
United Kingdom and France, 199
UP Asbestos Ltd., 72
UP Auto Tractors, 87
UP Cement Corp., 73, 87
UP State Cement Corp., (UPSCC),
66, 67, 69, 70, 73, 74, 75, 81, 82-
84
USA, 200, 201, 203
USSR and China, 201
Uttar Pradesh, 3, 5, 67, 146, 147,
148, 153, 154

W

Welfare Corp., 194
Welfare Enterprises, 4
West Bengal, 3, 4, 144
West Bengal and Kerala, 146, 147
West Europe, 201
West Germany, 200
World War I, 198, 200
WSLPEs, (Welfare SLPEs), 153,
154
Number, 153

□□□